Devin Booker: The Inspiring Story of One of Basketball's Rising Shooting Guards

An Unauthorized Biography

By: Clayton Geoffreys

Table of Contents

Foreword

Since entering the league in the 2015-2016 season, Devin Booker quickly emerged as a prominent shooting guard. By his second season, Booker was averaging 22.1 points at the young age of twenty. It's no surprise the Phoenix Suns extended a maximum five-year rookie extension worth $158 million to Booker in the summer of 2018 after just three seasons. Devin is one of the most prominent young scorers in the league today, consistent in his output and ability to create his own shots. The Suns got close to winning the NBA Championship in 2020-2021 season, winning the first two games in the seven-game series before losing out the rest of the way to the Milwaukee Bucks and a dominant Giannis Antetokounmpo. That said, the Suns reworked their roster a few years later, making a huge trade for Kevin Durant to chase their title aspirations. It'll be exciting to see what lies ahead for Devin Booker and the Suns. Thank you for purchasing *Devin Booker: The Inspiring Story of One of Basketball's Rising Shooting Guards*. In this unauthorized biography, we will learn Devin Booker's incredible life story and impact on the game of basketball. Hope you enjoy and if you do, please do not forget to leave a review!

Also, check out my website at claytongeoffreys.com to join my exclusive list where I let you know about my latest books. To thank you for your purchase, you can go to my site to download a free copy of *33 Life Lessons: Success Principles, Career Advice & Habits of Successful People*. In the book, you'll learn from some of the greatest thought leaders of different industries on what it takes to become successful and how to live a great life.

Cheers,

Clayton Geoffreys

Visit me at www.claytongeoffreys.com

Introduction

In today's NBA, there are two things about a player that will always get scouts, coaches, and general managers raving. No, we are not talking about experience or stats. We are talking about skills and potential. When those two aspects are abundantly evident in one prospect, it is almost impossible for any scout or coach to pass on that player. Time and time again, it has been proven that skilled players with potential will most likely end up not only as stars but also as game-changers.

In 1995, the Minnesota Timberwolves did not make a mistake when they drafted an 18-year-old Kevin Garnett straight out of high school, even though he had not played a single college game. We could also look at Kobe Bryant, who got passed on by 12 teams in 1996. Any of those teams, in retrospect, would have drafted him top overall had that draft been done over again. And we all know what happened in 2003 when 18-year-old phenom LeBron James was taken top overall. There is no need to expound on the career LeBron has carved out for himself since the teenager first stepped onto an NBA court.

Obviously, all of those players were drafted at a very young age. But age was not the only factor in why those teams took their chances when they drafted players that had not proven themselves in college. What was apparent was that they did not need to dominate in college because they already had enough potential to become stars in the NBA.

But young, talented players do not always make an easy transition to the professional leagues. While it only took until their second season in the league for Garnett, Bryant, and James to establish themselves as All-Stars, there have been some high school-to-pro players that did not become stars or realize their potential. Nevertheless, teams will always gamble on a young player with a lot of potential because they know that, if they can hone them the right way, they can eventually pay dividends.

Ever since the NBA implemented the rule that requires players to stay at least one year in college or overseas, there have not been many talented 18-year-olds coming into the NBA. More often than not, the top prospects have been one-and-done stars that have proven themselves as talented players in the single season they spent in college. In that sense, there is no longer a mystique when it comes to what these young college stars could do. Almost no one would wonder if they could translate their respective games to the NBA after doing well in college.

Despite playing a year in college, a young man named Devin Booker did not have the chance to dominate in Kentucky. Booker joined a very talented Kentucky Wildcats team as a 17-year-old. He was the youngest player on a team that already had a balanced offense. And because he had to play behind the older and more established veterans at the guard position, he never started a single game in college or had a chance to showcase his dominance.

Nevertheless, in 2015, Devin Booker took his chances and applied for the NBA Draft. Everybody knew that he was young. He was an 18-year-old player that had enjoyed a successful season in Kentucky despite playing off the bench. But the problem was that nobody saw that he had star potential. How could you possibly know?

Nevertheless, the Phoenix Suns took their chances with the young guard and drafted the 6'6" swingman with the 13th overall pick. As history has shown, the last 6'6", 18-year-old swingman that was drafted 13th overall turned out to become one of the greatest players to ever grace the NBA floor. Of course, Devin Booker was no Kobe Bryant, at least at that moment in time. But that still did not stop the Suns from drafting him for his youth and what seemed to be promising potential, albeit hidden underneath his youthful facade.

Playing for a young Phoenix Suns team that was in the process of rebuilding, Devin Booker now had a chance to finally show what he was made of. When the 18-year-old rookie showed flashes of the potential that 12 other teams had passed on in the 2015 NBA Draft, you could no longer miss it. He immediately established himself as a high-scoring guard that could become a franchise player if developed the right way.

When the Suns were looking for production, particularly with many of their backcourt men getting injured, Booker was there to pick up the slack. Known as a shooter in college, he showed his mettle as a steady playmaker. He could find open men within the flow of the system all while being the focal point of the offense as a player that could run off screens and knock down shots off the catch.

In his sophomore season in the NBA, Booker went on to prove himself as a quality franchise player. He would soon go on to become the Suns' leading scorer, and one of the youngest players to average 20 points per game in the history of the NBA. But he first made himself known to the world in March 2017, when he exploded for 70 points in a single game.

Joining Wilt Chamberlain, Elgin Baylor, David Robinson, David Thompson, and Kobe Bryant, Devin Booker became only the sixth player in league history to score at least 70 points in a single NBA game. And, at the tender age of 20, he became the *youngest* to do so. In fact, he also became the youngest player in league history to score at least 60 points. Indeed, Devin wasted no time putting his name in the record books and establishing himself as one of the premier young players in the league.

But Booker did not achieve such a feat by being the knockdown shooter he was regarded as back in college. He showed his brilliance as a ball-handler by getting his defenders off-balance with his dribbles. Booker also displayed his ability to create shots off the dribble and even attacked the basket, not only to get easier looks near the rim but to also draw fouls. It was a performance reminiscent of what Kobe Bryant did when he scored 81 points.

But that was not a one-hit-wonder of a performance for Booker. He used that career game to catapult himself into the spotlight, becoming a force that could one day end the Phoenix Suns' playoff drought. Since then, he has displayed his brilliance as an all-around scorer and capable playmaker. Devin Booker has indeed become one of the brightest young stars in today's NBA.

Booker quickly became a household name in the game when he captured fandom's attention, together with the upstart Phoenix Suns. He became a young All-Star at the age of 23. Then, in 2021, he led his Suns team to one of the top seeds in the entire league and went on to qualify for the NBA Finals for the first time in his career. And the leadership skills of Chris Paul rubbed off on him because he and his Suns were able to get all the way to the championship round.

Inspired by Kobe Bryant, Devin Booker had a magical playoff run in 2021 that allowed him to get within two wins of what could have been his first NBA championship at the age of 24. However, he and his Suns were defeated in six games by the Milwaukee Bucks, and Booker would need to go back to the drawing board to earn a chance at a return trip to the finals once more.

Ever since that run to the finals, Booker has become one of the true elites of the sport of basketball. He is one of the top shooting guards in the entire NBA. In 2022, he made first team All-NBA for the first time in his career, and this was the validation he needed to secure his place as one of the top wings the league had to offer. And he did so without the need to rely on athletic abilities and natural physical talents.

Truly one of the best scorers the NBA has to offer, Devin Booker still has a chance to redeem himself for that loss in the 2021 NBA Finals and assert himself as one of the greatest players in Phoenix Suns history. There are still a lot of great young players in the league, and Booker has yet to reach his prime. As such, he will undoubtedly be one of the poster boys of the league for years to come.

Chapter 1: Childhood and Early Life

Devin Armani Booker was born on October 30, 1996, in Grand Rapids, Michigan, to parents Veronica Gutierrez and Melvin Booker. He is of African-American, Mexican-American, and Puerto Rican descent. Basketball is also in his genetic background. Though Devin's mother was not a standout athlete, Melvin used to be a great ballplayer himself.

Melvin Booker was no slouch when it came to basketball. He was once a phenomenal talent in his hometown of Moss Point, Mississippi, and was even named Player of the Year as a senior. He then went on to play for Missouri in college and was named Conference Player of the Year in 1994 after averaging 18.1 points and 4.5 assists as a senior point guard.[i]

In 1995, Melvin found himself playing in the NBA for the two-time defending champions, the Houston Rockets. He only played 11 games for Houston and mostly played garbage minutes. He then moved to the Denver Nuggets during the 1996-97 season but was later traded to the Golden State Warriors in the middle of the year. He only played in 21 games that season. After that, he played for numerous international leagues while Veronica was at home taking care of young Devin.

Melvin met Veronica in Grand Rapids, Michigan, when his father was still playing in the CBA but before he got his chance in the NBA. About two years later, Devin was born, but Melvin had to go overseas to pursue an international basketball career. In fact, Devin's middle name was taken from the name of Melvin's basketball team (Armani) when he was in Italy. But Melvin always made it a point to go home whenever he could to help raise Devin to not only be a responsible citizen but also a future basketball star.

Though Melvin was an attentive father with the time he had for his family, that time was fairly minimal because of his career. Devin spent most of his childhood years under the wing of his mother Veronica. Seemingly like a single mother because Melvin was overseas earning for his family, Veronica had to raise Devin and his siblings on her own most of the time. Devin said that his mother never complained about it and was always positive about the situation the family was in.[ii]

Devin idolized his father even though he was often far away in Europe playing basketball. He worked hard on his basketball skills because he grew up loving the sport, and, of course, he wanted to be just like his dad. As Melvin would say, Devin was a gym rat, even as a child. He spent much of his time working on his game and honing his love and passion for basketball.[iii]

Devin Booker also spent some time in international gyms working with his father. When he was young, he always asked his mother to allow him to go to Russia where Melvin was initially playing. However, Veronica never allowed him to go overseas until Melvin began playing in Italy. When his father was in Italy, Devin went with him during games and practices.

Devin recalled one of the best moments of his childhood when he got to play one-on-one with Danilo Gallinari, who was yet to make it to the NBA at that time. Booker was just 12 years old at the time, but he did his best against the Italian professional player because he was motivated by the fact that his father was also a pro.

As a pro, Melvin taught Devin a lot about the game that only professional basketball players can ever know. He taught his son the importance of developing a high IQ for basketball because that was how a player could make up for any lack of athletic ability. At that point, Devin already knew that he did not have the highest athletic potential but he made up for his lack of speed and leaping ability with his knowledge and feel for the game.[iv]

Melvin Booker retired from basketball in 2008 and moved back to the United States for good. At that time, 12-year-old Devin was still developing as a young middle school star, and even played with and against fellow future NBA player D'Angelo Russell and future Kentucky teammate Tyler Ulis. But Devin was about to make a crucial decision in his life.

Shortly after playing in Michigan for Grandville High School's freshman team, Devin followed his father and moved to Melvin's hometown of Moss Point, Mississippi. Having just retired from basketball, Melvin was hired by his hometown high school as an assistant coach. Wanting to be with his father, Devin enrolled in Moss Point High School where he eventually became a star.

Chapter 2: High School Career

Devin Booker always says that moving to Mississippi was what changed his basketball career for the better. However, at first, Veronica Gutierrez almost did not allow Devin to move in with his father. Melvin was also hesitant because he did not want to become the reason for separating a young teenager from his mother. But he eventually convinced himself, Devin, and Veronica that this was what was needed for the younger Booker to progress as a player.[v]

With that decision finalized, Devin Booker moved to Moss Point, Mississippi, in 2011. But it was not an easy transition for him to move a thousand miles away from home. It was an entirely different environment for him and he did not have friends in Moss Point. He hardly knew anybody other than his father. But Melvin helped make the transition easier for Devin. More importantly, he was there to help hone his son's basketball talent.

Because Melvin was there to help the sophomore high school player, Devin Booker became an instant prep sensation. In just his fifth game of the season for Moss Point, Devin already established himself as the team's brightest young star after scoring more points than any of his teammates combined. He also had several other phenomenal, high-scoring games as well as game-winning buzzer-beaters. In just his sophomore year in high school, Booker was averaging over 23 points per game.

He made a splash that season when he went for a ridiculous scoring performance in the MLK Classic of that year. Booker scored 54 points and was only 9 points shy of the school record of 63 points that was set well over two decades ago.[vi] At such a young age, the 6'4" guard was already doing things that were not expected of a sophomore.

Melvin Booker said that Devin seemed ahead of his time despite his young age. But Devin said that it was all thanks to how his father guided him throughout his sophomore year (and first season) at Moss Point. The younger Booker gave his father the praise he deserved for being the guiding voice that made him understand the things only professional basketball players know.

Describing his father as someone who "knows all the tricks and traits of the game," Devin believed that having a dad or guiding figure that had been through the usual process of getting to the professional ranks was something every young player needed.[v] It was not only Melvin's knowledge as a professional point guard but also the vast experience he gathered all over the world that got Devin Booker to where he was at such a young age.

Nevertheless, Melvin still said that his son's natural talent and acumen were what helped him become such a young high school star. Just turning 15 years old, Devin could already understand things that college players were still trying to learn. Melvin said that it was all because of his son's intelligence and ability to absorb information at a high level.[v]

It also helped that both father and son breathed basketball and never stopped talking or thinking about it. They would watch games together and try to dissect plays and strategies together. It was a bonding moment that translated into player development on the part of Devin Booker. Of course, they were both happy with that arrangement.

By the time Devin became a junior, he used his intelligence to his full advantage when he was moved to the point guard position. He began that year with a bang. The 16-year-old guard went for 29 points in his first game of the season. Then, in December of 2012, he even outscored an entire team all by himself through three quarters when he scored 40 points while the opposing squad only had 39 entering the fourth quarter.

With performances such as those, Devin was showing that he was already learning how to create shots and score off the dribble like a point guard or a primary ball-handler rather than merely being content as a spot-up shooter. He was so good as a junior that he got the press raving about his innate talent on both ends of the court. He was described as a high-energy player that could impose his will on both offense and defense.[vii]

Later that month in the Jackie Laird Christmas Classic, Devin Booker scored a season-high 49 points, a performance that got college programs turning their heads toward the young combo guard. At that point, Michigan was already trying to get their hands on Devin. But Duke was paying attention as well and became a front-runner after that 49-point explosion that Booker delivered in the tournament.[viii]

Even University of Missouri fans went on to cheer for Devin Booker in a tournament held in Missouri. Knowing that his father, Melvin Booker, was once the school's best player two decades ago, the Tiger fans roared for the younger Booker trying to entice him to follow in his father's footsteps. The 6'5" Devin Booker was averaging over 30 points per game in that tournament and did not disappoint.

At the end of the 2012-13 season, Devin Booker averaged 30 points, 8 rebounds, and 4 assists. He was named the best player of the division despite his team's mediocre record that season. He even got named the *Sun Herald*'s Player of the Year for a second consecutive season and was also Mississippi's Player of the Year. At that point, he was a widely-recruited player and was given a four-star ranking by *Rivals*. He was even named the top prospect in Mississippi and was nationally regarded by *Rivals* as the 30th-best player in the recruitment class of 2014.

But despite already having scholarship offers from Duke, Michigan, Florida, North Carolina, Missouri, and several other great college programs, Devin only got an offer from Kentucky's John Calipari during a youth camp in April of 2013 when he saw the young Moss Point star play for the first time. Calipari, who has had the pleasure of coaching the likes of Derrick Rose, John Wall, Anthony Davis, and DeMarcus Cousins, was impressed by what he saw.

When asked how he got to that point in his young career, Devin Booker said that it was thanks to how he learned the importance of working hard. He was always a talented basketball player that did not have to work hard to become a strong prospect. But what brought him to the dance was putting in the extra work, which was something he did not understand before his father taught him how valuable it was for a talented player to work harder than everyone else.[vi]

Indeed, Devin worked harder. During the summer before his senior year, he attended several elite skills camps that were hosted by NBA superstars such as LeBron James, Chris Paul, and Kevin Durant. He also took part in exclusive tournaments held for the best high school basketball players not only in the United States but on a global scale as well. It was like Devin was hustling and working hard to earn a spot on the varsity team even though he was already the state's best prep player.

But Devin Booker proved that his mettle as a player was not confined to Mississippi alone. In a game against the top-rated high school team in the country during the Marshall County Hoop Fest, Devin Booker exploded for 40 points despite the loss. A few days later, he then went for a 45-point output against another well-known high school program.

Then, in January of 2014, Devin Booker made Moss Point High School history by becoming the program's all-time scoring leader after going for 38 points in a win. At that point, it was already difficult to argue to the contrary how good of a high school star he was. He was already the school's greatest player and was arguably at the top of the list of Mississippi's all-time players.

During his senior year, Devin Booker averaged 31 points and tallied a total of 2,518 career points for the program. He finished high school as a four-star player according to *Rivals* and as a five-star player according to *ESPN*, who loved him so much that they wanted to televise the announcement of where he ultimately decided to play college basketball.

Speaking of colleges, it was during October of 2013 that Devin Booker decided on his school of choice. Despite the offer from *ESPN* to televise that decision, he opted not to because he did not want to be pressured. Instead, he made the decision in Moss Point's gymnasium and announced to the world that he was ready to commit to Kentucky.

It was a difficult decision to make for Devin, especially considering that he had the opportunity to go back to his hometown in Michigan or to follow in his father's footsteps in Missouri as the school's next great Booker. However, the decision to go to Kentucky was purely for basketball reasons. Certainly, he want to continue the legacy Melvin Booker had carved from Moss Point all the way to Missouri, but Kentucky had something that Missouri did not: John Calipari.

Devin Booker's decision to go to Kentucky was primarily because of John Calipari and the school's recent history as a successful program. John Calipari was a bona fide legend by this time and had made a name for himself as a college coach that helped develop future NBA stars. His long list of NBA All-Stars whom he has mentored includes Derrick Rose (an MVP winner himself), DeMarcus Cousins, John Wall, and Anthony Davis. And while they may not have become All-Stars, players such as Marcus Camby, Tyreke Evans, Eric Bledsoe, and Brandon Knight have all become successful NBA players under his tutelage themselves. And ever since the NBA started the one-and-done rule, John Calipari has proven that he could produce players that were already prepared for the NBA even after just one year in college.

Booker also said that he loved how Calipari showed how he could thrive under his system. The coach proved to Booker that he would flourish under his wing as a big guard that had the green light to shoot, which was Devin's primary weapon of choice. Although it was still a difficult decision to make, Melvin said that he did not have a hand in Devin's choice. He did not force him to go to Missouri and allowed him to make his own decision as a mature young man.[ix]

But before going to Kentucky, Devin Booker had one last hurrah as a high school player when he attended several elite basketball tournaments during the summer. He participated in the 2014 McDonald's All-American Game where he scored eight points. He then went on to play for the Jordan Brand Classic before dominating as the MVP in a Mississippi All-Star Game.

Chapter 3: College Career

Although he was a high school star in Mississippi, Booker became just another big fish in an even bigger pond when he joined a star-studded Kentucky Wildcats program. He was not even the school's prized recruit, as Kentucky had also secured the services of Karl-Anthony Towns together with two other freshman stars, namely Trey Lyles and Tyler Ulis. And because Kentucky also had veteran players such as the Harrison twins, it was expected that Booker was going to play off the bench. But that did not stop Booker from continuing to work hard. He knew that he had what it took to become an NBA star. And he also had plenty of patience.

Turning 18 that season, Devin was the youngest guy on the team but seemingly played with the wits and decision-making ability of a seasoned basketball veteran. He did not even complain about his role as the team's designated first guy off the bench but instead used it as a way to prove how truly explosive a shooter and scorer he was when those opportunities came his way.

Despite starting his college career with an 0-for-6 shooting performance against Grand Canyon, Devin Booker did not stop shooting. In his next game, he went for 10 points against Buffalo. Then, on November 21st, he went for 15 points on 5 out of 8 shooting versus Boston University. He followed that performance up with 18 and 19 points respectively against Montana State and Texas-Arlington.

On December 20th, in a nationally-televised game against UCLA, Devin Booker gained the nation's attention by matching his career high of 19 points when he made 7 of his 10 shots from the field. He then started 2015 right by going for 13 and 18 points respectively against Ole Miss and Texas A&M. And on January 24th, he exploded for 18 points on a 6 out of 9 shooting clip against South Carolina.

Booker would match that January 24th performance when he went for 18 points against Tennessee on February 17th. He then scored in double digits the next three games as Kentucky was proving itself as the powerhouse of college basketball. Booker helped his school get to the conference tournament undefeated in the 30 games he played for the team.

Since Kentucky once again dominated the conference tournament the same way they dominated the entire season, the Wildcats were entering the NCAA Tournament as an undefeated team through 34 consecutive games. Booker, who was not known as a winner in college, helped Kentucky earn a top overall spot.

In the second-round matchup between Kentucky and Hampton, Booker had a poor outing with only two points. Nevertheless, the Wildcats came out of that round with a win. Booker still struggled in their next outing when Kentucky met Cincinnati in the Round of 32. He only had six points but the Wildcats still dominated their way to an appearance in the next round.

In Kentucky's 39-point win over West Virginia in the Sweet 16, Booker bounced back to go for 12 points and 4 rebounds in the 17 minutes he played. The Wildcats were still undefeated heading into the Elite Eight, where they barely defeated Notre Dame. Devin Booker scored well enough to help his team win and finished that game with 10 points.

Though the Kentucky Wildcats were coming into the Final Four as the heavy favorites to win the National Championship, Wisconsin gave them a tough fight. Booker was hampered by the defense and could only score six points as the Wisconsin Badgers completed the upset over the formerly undefeated Kentucky Wildcats.

After just one season with the Kentucky Wildcats, Devin Booker averaged 10 points, 2 rebounds, and 1.1 assists in the 21 minutes he played. He never started a single game in the 38 times he suited up for the 38-1 Kentucky Wildcats team. While his stats and numbers do not seem too impressive for a highly-touted high school recruit, he stood out in what was a very balanced Kentucky attack.

Throughout Kentucky's 39 games, John Calipari stressed the importance of ball movement and balanced scoring. None of his players attempted more than 10 shots per game and seven players averaged at least 20 minutes a night. Despite such a balanced system, Booker stood out as the scoring punch the bench needed. He was the team's third-leading scorer behind Aaron Harrison's 11 points per game and Karl-Anthony Towns' 10.3 points per game. He did all that while playing off the bench and not seeing as many touches and shot attempts as he wanted to.

Devin Booker was so good in college that, years after he crossed over to the NBA, John Calipari said he might have held the young 18-year-old back from showing his entire offensive arsenal.[x] Booker, who won the SEC Sixth Man of the Year Award, only took 7.6 shots per game for the Wildcats. Imagine what could have happened had Booker been allowed to take twice as many shots as he did.

But Devin Booker never complained about his lack of touches (and neither did any of his teammates) because he, Calipari, and everyone on the team knew that sharing the ball was what they needed to do to dominate the collegiate ranks. Even top big man prospect Karl-Anthony Towns averaged under seven shots a night but was still good enough to get the attention of the entire world. It was an unselfish team that was taught well by the coaching staff. And while they may have come up short of winning the NCAA title, Booker and everyone else on that team knew that they needed to work together to achieve what was almost an undefeated season.

Devin used that one year in college as a stepping stone to his ultimate goal—making it to the NBA. Though he was still young enough to spend at least one more year in college to hone his talents and improve his draft stock by putting up better stats than he did in his freshman year, Booker was already prepared to try his hand at the biggest league in the world.

Chapter 4: NBA Career

Getting Drafted

Devin Booker and six other Kentucky Wildcats players expressed their desire to enter the 2015 NBA Draft. Because of this, Kentucky seemed like an entirely new team heading in the 2015-16 season, but they were proud to see seven of their products (Towns, Booker, Cauley-Stein, Lyles, Johnson, and the Harrison twins) moving on to the NBA.

The draft class of 2015 had a particularly talented pool of players that were vying for their own respective NBA spots. Among those players, Kentucky center Karl-Anthony Towns stood out because of what seemed like an unlimited pool of potential on both ends of the court. There was almost no arguing that he was the top pick of that year's NBA draft.

Meanwhile, another Kentucky big man was also garnering national attention. Willie Cauley-Stein, a junior, proved himself capable enough to attract NBA scouts and GMs. He was regarded as a lottery pick that had a chance to get taken in the top five. With two players regarded as top-10 picks, Kentucky showed that they were a program that could produce some of the best NBA prospects.

But, where was Devin Booker in the conversation?

Weirdly enough, Booker was not getting much attention coming into the draft, even though there were not many talented guards in that class. Guards such as D'Angelo Russell, Mario Hezonja, and Emmanuel Mudiay were getting more attention than he was. Was it because he did not prove himself as a productive player when he was with Kentucky? Or was it due to other factors?

When looking at what Booker could do on the floor, it was understandable that he was compared to the likes of Klay Thompson and Gordon Hayward because he was a knockdown shooter at the wing position. His physical attributes were also comparable to those two players, who would later become All-Stars.

At 6'6" and 205 pounds, Devin Booker had the right size for a wing player that could play both the shooting guard and small forward positions. And when it came to athletic ability, he also resembled Thompson and Hayward. He is not a particularly fast runner or high leaper but his overall athleticism is not a weak part of his game.

Offensively, Booker was a brilliant operator that could knock jumpers down without much effort. He had one of the quickest strokes and releases in college and a form that checked almost perfectly concerning mechanics and smoothness.[xi] It is almost as if he was born to shoot the ball because, at the young age of 18, he could already knock down shots faster and with a more balanced form than some ten-year NBA veterans.

But while Booker was already shooting jumpers effortlessly and with a follow-through reminiscent of some of the greatest shooters in league history, it was *how* he got those jump shots up that was so impressive. No matter the angle or distance, Booker could always shoot his jumpers in the same consistent and balanced form. And because of his high release point, it was almost impossible to block his jump shot.

But Devin was always more than just a spot-up shooter. He could get his jumpers up off the screen much like how J.J. Redick does. He could also create enough space for his jump shot whenever he attacked off the dribble. He could either pull his shot up or take a step back to create more space. Shooting was always the part of the game that he excelled at. That was why he was shooting more than 41% at the college three-point line when he was with Kentucky.

Devin Booker's body control translates well whenever he is attacking the basket. At his size, he can finish impressively near the rim by contorting his body or absorbing impact in such a way that he does not lose his balance up in the air. He is not the most athletic shooting guard, but he knows how to get the job done with that terrific body control he possesses.

As a rebounder and defender, Devin Booker mostly gets by with effort and IQ rather than with his innate abilities. He did not get the most steals and blocks at his position when he was with Kentucky, but he was never a defensive liability. He was always a smart defender and timely rebounder, even in high school. He simply knew how to maximize what his physical tools allowed him to do.

Aside from his ability to shoot, it was Devin Booker's intangibles that got scouts excited about this prospect. At 18 years old, Booker already had the instincts, discipline, and unselfishness of a seasoned NBA veteran. He already knew what his role was and what he needed to do to get the best shots possible. Whether it was moving well without the ball ala Klay Thompson, spreading the floor to provide driving lanes for guards, filling the lanes correctly on the break, or putting pressure on his defensive assignment, Devin Booker always seemed to know the right things to do on the court.

As Melvin Booker said, Devin was always a smart young man that understood basketball in a more advanced way than any of his peers. It was as if his brain and IQ were wired to absorb basketball information and knowledge like a sponge. His maturity for an 18-year-old player was similar to that of LeBron's when he was just a rookie. However, there were some reasons why Booker was not a highly-touted prospect.

While he does have the proper size for someone that could play both wing positions, Booker is not an impressive physical specimen. He did not have the strength to physically punish his matchup on both ends of the floor. And as the NBA increasingly becomes a league with some of the most athletic men on the planet, Booker was neither the fastest runner nor the highest leaper. He could not wow anyone with his athletic abilities.

For someone that stood 6'6", he also seemed smaller than he actually was because he did not have a particularly long wingspan or a strong, muscular build. His body does not even look like it could handle a few more pounds of lean weight. Booker also did not have an explosive first step that would have made up for his lack of foot speed.[xi]

On the scoring end, Devin Booker had a ball-handling ability that was acceptable at the college level but was probably not up to par in the NBA. Despite showing the ability to create space for his shots back in Kentucky, there was no assurance that he could transform into a good shooter and shot-maker off the dribble against the more elite defenses in the NBA.[xii]

Although Booker has shown the ability to make shots near the basket because of his terrific body control, he seemed to struggle to finish at the basket because he just did not have the necessary explosiveness, length, and strength to challenge big men. Almost 90% of the shots he took in college were jump shots and there were only a handful of isolation plays drawn up for him.[xii]

There was also a problem with how Devin struggled as a half-court player on the drives. Most of his finishes near the basket were coming off transition plays. Other than that, he usually struggled to get all the way to the basket and mostly finished off floaters and short-range jumpers. He also had a tendency to lose his touch whenever defenses got too physical with him.

Defensively, Devin Booker may not be a lazy defender, but he still is not regarded as a decent one, despite putting in the necessary effort on that end of the floor. It was never because he was just a bad defender or someone that did not put in the work on that end of the floor, but it was because he did not appear to have all the physical tools needed to become a truly elite player on that end of the floor.

Despite standing 6'6", he does not have a high standing reach or a long wingspan. In fact, players that have a standing reach that is 8'4" or lower are mostly smaller shooting guards. Most wing players tend to have the length and reach to do fairly well on the defensive end. But despite his height, Booker would most likely struggle to contest shots because he seemed to lack the physical tools that could ultimately elevate that part of his game.

And when he was asked to defend off the ball, he sometimes seemed to struggle when trying to keep up with his assignment. This was not because he is not a very athletic player, but because he lacked the strength to fight through screens. He also had a bad habit of putting his body on his defender to make up for his lack of lateral quickness. That would most likely result in fouls in the NBA, especially considering that the guards in the big league are so quick and explosive.[xi]

Because of these perceived weaknesses, some scouts that believed Devin Booker would merely end up as a role player who stretched the floor and pressured the defense with his ability to shoot while spotting up or coming off screens. But those critics hardly believed that he had the makings of a player that could score off the bounce or near the basket. Doubters thought that he would only end up as a serviceable player like J.J. Redick, Kirk Hinrich, or Randy Foye. Meanwhile, the most positive scouts saw greater potential. They thought he could become the next Klay Thompson.

But because the NBA was becoming increasingly reliant on the three-point shot, Devin Booker was a no-risk player. He could easily end up as a valuable asset for any team in the NBA. Even if he did not have the makings of a superstar, he was clearly a guy that knew what his role for the team was. It was probably going to be like what he did for Kentucky when he did what was asked of him.

Despite all of those projections, what scouts could not quantify was Devin Booker's intangibles. He had quality aspects such as his innate basketball IQ, impressive intelligence, and dedication to the sport. In fact, he was so dedicated to basketball that he spent a lot of time watching film. And most of the videos he watched were about Klay Thompson.

Known strictly as a shooter back in college, Klay Thompson was not a very highly touted prospect coming into his draft because of his lack of athleticism and off-the-dribble scoring ability. However, he has since transformed himself into the NBA's most dangerous off-the-ball scorer and one of the best perimeter wing defenders on the planet.

Booker knew how hard Klay had worked on his game and how he has developed into a dangerous two-way player that commanded the respect of any NBA defense.[xiii] He saw that Thompson was the blueprint he needed to follow, not only as a shooter but also as a player seeking to improve on the defensive end. But what was scary about Booker was that he was only 18 years old coming into the draft. Klay Thompson was a 21-year-old junior when he got to the NBA. That was the biggest reason why Devin could turn out to be a hidden gem for any team.

When draft day came, the inevitable came true when Karl-Anthony Towns, Booker's Kentucky teammate, was drafted by the Minnesota Timberwolves. The first guard taken in the draft was D'Angelo Russell, who was picked by the Lakers. Guards Emmanuel Mudiay and Mario Hezonja were both taken in the lottery. Meanwhile, Willie Cauley-Stein, another Kentucky product, was taken sixth.

It was a fruitful draft for Kentucky when Trey Lyles was taken 12th overall by the Utah Jazz. That pick meant that three Kentucky players were drafted before Devin. But he did not have to wait long because he was then promptly taken by the Phoenix Suns with the 13th overall pick of the 2015 NBA Draft.

While nobody thought that the Phoenix Suns had found their next franchise star when they drafted Devin Booker, it was clear that they had made the best choice when they took the 18-year-old. He was predicted to become a serviceable player for the Phoenix Suns' ball-dominant backcourt duo. But nobody thought he was going to be a starter or even a player that could produce right away.

Nevertheless, Devin Booker was already on his way to proving that he was going to be better than the player everyone thought he would be. After all, the last 18-year-old shooting guard taken 13th overall turned out to be good enough to become a five-time champion and an MVP.

Rookie Season

When Devin Booker joined the Phoenix Suns, he was the youngest player in the league, and the youngest to play on an NBA team since they established the rule that required prospects to play at least one year in college. At first, it appeared as if Booker was set to become a project player because of his youth. However, the Phoenix Suns were in dire need of production, especially because they were desperately trying to get back to playoff contention.

The NBA is always evolving. At that time, the NBA had grown dependent on the three-point shot and on what point guards could do. Though the top players in the league were forwards, point guards were increasingly becoming more important than they ever were because of how well they fit the league's emphasis on a faster pace and better floor spacing. This was why top point guards such as

Stephen Curry, Kyrie Irving, and Russell Westbrook were thriving and dominating in their own way.

Even shooting guards were finding their own niche in the league. Though he was not your traditional shooting guard, James Harden's ability to make plays and shoot three-pointers made him one of the league's premier superstars. And Klay Thompson, who normally would not have become a star because of his lack of athleticism, was considered the top two-way shooting guard in the league because of his amazing and historic three-point shooting prowess and in-your-face defense.

As the league transitioned into a pace-and-space era run by guards that had both speed and shooting, the Phoenix Suns utilized a backcourt run by two point guards. Their starters were Eric Bledsoe and Kentucky and Calipari product Brandon Knight. The Suns hoped that their two-point guard lineup would work well in a fast-paced run-and-gun system. And with Devin Booker backing the guards up, they had a capable outside shooter off the bench.

Normally, nobody would consider Devin Booker as a potential go-to guy for any team. After all, he did not have the ball-handling capabilities of James Harden and was not as quick and athletic as Russell Westbrook. But because of how the NBA has evolved, the possibility of him becoming a star was not a farfetched idea because of how Klay Thompson and Stephen Curry, both of whom were not physically blessed, developed to become great players and champions.

And considering how Booker proved himself in the NBA Summer League by averaging 15 points per game, it was becoming apparent that he was better than advertised.

Devin Booker made his official NBA debut on October 28, 2015, against the Dallas Mavericks. He had an impressive outing in the first game by going for 14 points on 6 out of 7 shooting from the field while playing 21 minutes in that loss. He made history that night by becoming the first player to play an NBA game at age 18 during the one-and-done era.

But because the Phoenix Suns were giving more minutes and touches to older and more experienced guards, Devin Booker hardly played in the next eight games. And if he did play, he did not have enough looks, opportunities, or touches to prove how good he really was. Nevertheless, he still performed well when he was given the chance.

On November 22nd, Devin Booker went for a new career high. In a loss to the New Orleans Pelicans, the newly-turned 19-year-old went for 15 points on 5 out of 8 shooting from the field. Even more impressively, he achieved that in only 16 minutes of play off the bench. That performance helped him earn more minutes as a backup guard for the rebuilding and struggling Phoenix Suns.

Booker would soon once again eclipse his career high in points. On December 2nd, he played 23 minutes off the bench and made all three of his three-pointers and 5 of his 6 shots from the field to finish the game with 18 points. Proving that such a performance was not a fluke, five days later, he earned starter minutes off the bench and went for 14 points and 5 assists in a win over the Chicago Bulls. But again, Booker went back to his regular role as a solid backup guard that played inconsistent minutes off the bench.

On December 26th, Booker would break his career high to tie the most points he put up when he was at Kentucky. In almost 20 minutes off the bench in a loss to the Philadelphia 76ers, Booker hit 6 of his 11 shots from the field and 3 of his 4 three-pointers to score 19 points. That performance and the injury to Eric Bledsoe on the same night earned him the role he would hold onto for the rest of his career.

After not starting a single official game for almost two seasons, ever since he joined Kentucky in 2014, Devin Booker was finally elevated to the role of starting shooting guard on December 28th to replace Eric Bledsoe in the lineup. In the 29 minutes he played against the Cleveland Cavaliers on the day he was given the starting position for good, Booker finished with 10 points, 3 rebounds, and 3 assists. Before getting the starting nod, he was only averaging five points as a backup guard.

Getting elevated to the starting position gave Devin the touches and opportunities to shine that he needed to prove that he was better than the role player most scouts thought he would end up as. On January 2, 2016, he went for another career high when he shot 6 out of 10 from the field and 7 out of 8 from the free-throw line to score 21 points in a loss to the Sacramento Kings. He became the sixth-youngest player to score at least 20 points in a single game. Stars such as Kobe Bryant, Tracy McGrady, LeBron James, Dwight Howard, and Kevin Durant were the only players to score 20 or more points at a younger age than when Booker did.

Then, four days later in a win over the Charlotte Hornets, Booker went for his first double-double game since high school by finishing with 17 points and 10 rebounds. Only LeBron James, Giannis Antetokounmpo, Michael Kidd-Gilchrist, and Andrew Bynum were younger when they recorded their first double-double performance.

After that, on January 19th, Devin Booker would again go for an explosive performance to put up a new career high in points. In that three-point loss to the Indiana Pacers, the 19-year-old shooting guard finished with 32 points on 9 out of 16 shooting from the field and 6 out of 11 shooting from the three-point line. He not only made the most three-pointers ever by a Suns rookie, but he also became the third-youngest player to score at least 30 points in a single game. He is behind only LeBron James and Kevin Durant in that achievement.

Devin Booker did not slow down after that first 30-point performance. He continued to score in double digits and even more than 20 points on certain occasions. In fact, he went for 11 consecutive double-digit scoring performances from January 17th to February 6th. He averaged 19.3 points on 43% shooting from the field and 40.6% shooting from the three-point line during that run. And ever since he became a starter, he was averaging 17 points, 3.3 rebounds, and 2.5 assists through his first 20 starts for the Phoenix Suns.

On February 10th, he matched up well with Klay Thompson, a player he idolized, to put up a great all-around game. In that loss to the Golden State Warriors, he had a particularly good performance against the defending champions and Thompson when he finished the game with 15 points, 10 assists, and 7 rebounds for a near triple-double.

Devin Booker entered the midseason break as a hot rookie that was earning the attention and praise of the entire NBA. He participated in the 2016 Rising Stars Challenge as a member of Team USA. He helped his team win a close battle by going for 23 points on 5 out of 8 shooting from the three-point line off the bench. Then, a day later, he participated in the Three-Point Contest to become the youngest player to take part in that event. At 19 years old, Devin Booker was doing things no scout thought he could do when he was a draft prospect. It was becoming apparent that he was the steal of the 2015 NBA Draft.

Using his first All-Star Weekend experience as a way to catapult himself into the spotlight, Booker was looking more confident than ever in the second half of the season. On March 3rd, he eclipsed his career high in points when he went for 34 on 11 out of 21 shooting from the field in a loss to the Miami Heat. Only three players in league history have ever recorded multiple 30-point games in a single season younger than when Booker did.

Six days later, Booker recorded his third 30-point game of the season when he went for 32 points on 14 out of 28 shooting from the field in a loss to the New York Knicks. But that was not the end of his explosive performances because it only took a day for him to eclipse his career high in points.

On March 10th, Devin Booker finished a loss to the Denver Nuggets with a new career high in points. He finished that outing with 35 points on 12 out of 24 shooting from the field. And proving that he had developed into a crafty player that could fish for fouls, he made 10 of his 11 free throws in that outing.

Two days after that career performance, Booker would go for his third double-double of the season when he finished a loss to the Golden State Warriors with 18 points and 11 assists. He then continued to play exceptionally well as the Phoenix Suns' brightest spot in what was an otherwise gloomy season filled with injuries and disappointing losses.

On March 28th, Booker went for his fifth 30-point game of the season when he finished a loss to the Minnesota Timberwolves with 30 points on 10 out of 22 shooting from the field. Then, just when the season was about to end, he turned in a performance that was just one point short of tying his career high in points. Booker had 34 points on 12 out of 24 shooting from the field in that loss to the Atlanta Hawks.

Devin Booker truly had an incredible second half of the season. In the 28 games that followed the All-Star Weekend, he averaged 19.2

points, 3 rebounds, and 4.1 assists. Proving that he was not only a shooter, he also averaged 4.7 free-throw attempts during that run. Since February 19th, he scored in single digits only twice.

Finishing a successful and surprisingly impressive rookie season, Booker averaged 13.8 points, 2.5 rebounds, and 2.6 assists. He was making 42.3% of his shots from the field and 34.3% of his attempts from the three-point line. He was averaging 18 points per game from the time he was given the starting spot on December 28, 2015. Had he been a starter from the beginning, he could have been the top scorer among all the rookies that season.

Nevertheless, Devin Booker earned high praise from coaches and peers after that incredible rookie campaign. He got so much respect that he was voted into the All-Rookie 1st Team. Booker also finished fourth in votes for the Rookie of the Year Award. His Kentucky teammate Karl-Anthony Towns was named Rookie of the Year that season.

With the way Devin Booker turned his season around when he got the starting nod and touches he needed, he proved the doubters wrong and showed the world that he was probably worth a top-five spot back in the 2015 NBA Draft. Underestimated as only a pure shooter who would end up as a role player, Devin Booker was surprising almost everyone and displaying flashes of star potential and brilliance. And not only that but the 19-year-old rookie phenom was quickly becoming the new face of the Phoenix Suns.

But how exactly did he get to that point at such a young age?

In their most honest words, not even the Phoenix Suns' front office expected the youngest player in the NBA to go out and become the crucial on-the-ball scorer and playmaker that he transformed into in his rookie season. The Suns' GM thought that Booker would just play like a traditional shooting guard that would shoot jumpers off passes from their point guards' penetrations or off the screen. Instead, Devin Booker was demonstrating that he was a lot better than advertised.

When both Eric Bledsoe and Brandon Knight missed time because of injuries, the Phoenix Suns had no one else to turn to for playmaking. That was when Devin Booker came in. He had to play the role of the team's playmaker, even though he had spent most of his life as a wing player playing off the ball. Already proving himself as a capable off-the-ball scorer, Booker showed his prowess as a primary ball-handler.

The 19-year-old shooting guard was running pick-and-roll plays like a shooting guard that had to play the role of a de facto point guard much like James Harden. Though he was yet to reach the level of craftiness and ball-handling skills that Harden had, he was making intelligent plays for both himself and his teammates. The shooting guard was already showing a unique feel for the game that not even rookie point guards had.

When running the pick-and-roll, Devin always knew what to do. He could freeze defenders up with his dribble and make big men think twice about switching to him to challenge his shot off the dribble because he was also an unselfish player that knew when to pass out to a cutting teammate whenever opponents tried to close out on him. It was more of a function of how high his basketball IQ was and how he could make decisions on the fly instead of how scary of a ball-handler or shooter he was.

Booker credited his high basketball IQ and knowledge to his father, who was once a capable point guard himself. Instead of trying to outrun and outjump opponents that were always superior athletes, Booker used his inherited intelligence and feel for the game to make the best basketball decisions and to try to become the smartest player on the hardwood floor.[iv]

The most beautiful thing about it was that Booker was not putting up empty stats as the de facto best player on a team ravaged and depleted by injuries. Instead, he was using the injuries and increased minutes and possessions as an opportunity to explode onto the scene much earlier than expected. And learned coaches and basketball enthusiasts know that Booker's stats were not a product of the Suns desperately trying to look for production. In fact, some would even agree that he was already a better playmaker than starting guard Brandon Knight.[iv]

Earl Watson, who was the Suns' head coach back then, said that they already saw that Booker was more than just a spot-up player back in his brilliant tournament performances in the NBA Summer League. However, he also said that Booker was not as good back then as he was in the latter half of the regular season. He had grown in versatility and decision-making in a span of just a few months. That was a testament to how hard Booker worked on his game.

From a player that was merely scoring off the catch in Kentucky to an improved scorer during the Summer League, Booker has evolved into an intelligent player that can play just as well on the ball as he does off it. He has learned how to navigate himself through screens and lose his defenders by getting them off-balanced through his intelligent study of film and plays. And because of his quick release, all he needs is to make his opponent think that he going one way while going to another spot on the floor to get himself open for a split second and to shoot the lightning-quick shot that he has always had.

Nevertheless, at that point, the Phoenix Suns were not quick to put Devin Booker high up on a pedestal as a legitimate first option on the scoring end. He had proven himself far better than advertised but he still had many things to learn before he could truly become one of the best players in the league. And with Eric Bledsoe and Brandon Knight returning the next season, it was difficult to project what his role would be once the Suns were completely healthy.

Other than that, the Phoenix Suns' coaches were well aware that Booker still needed to grow on the defensive end. He was, after all, still more-or-less an inexperienced rookie that was still trying to adjust against the more physical, athletic, and advanced NBA offenses. In that regard, Booker was among the worst defenders in the league at his position. But it was not because of a lack of effort on his part. His coaches saw that the teenager was processing the opponents' offensive sets but he had trouble catching up due to his inexperience and lack of physical abilities.

As Earl Watson said, offenses in the NBA are about patterns.[iv] As a defender, a player must be able to see these patterns and learn how to react accordingly. The best way for a player to learn these patterns on the defensive end is through experience. But as a 19-year-old rookie, he was still lacking in the experience department.

The coaching staff also knew how badly Booker struggled fighting over the top of the screens and keeping in step with his defenders because he lacked strength.[iv] With that in mind, adding strength and muscle was one of the things Devin Booker needed to do during the offseason so that he could improve not only as a defender, but as a scorer.

All that said, it was easy to surmise that Booker was not going to spend his entire career as a poor defender. At worst, he would be on par with average defenders. He could even potentially become a great one because of his effort, balance, and maniacal dedication to improving his craft. He was already showing that he could keep track of the opponents' offensive sets. All Booker needed to do was grow mentally and physically on that end of the floor.

But even if he did grow drastically on both ends of the floor, there were still questions about what his future role with the team was going to be, especially because the Phoenix Suns had already invested heavily in their quick and spitfire backcourt. Eric Bledsoe and Brandon Knight were still quality players in their own right, and they also had experience on their side. And on top of that, there was still the possibility that Devin Booker's rookie season was just a fluke.

Nevertheless, if the Phoenix Suns wanted to make the most out of Devin Booker's glaring potential and learn the true extent of what he could do, they should start him and play either Eric Bledsoe or Brandon Knight off the bench. But because Bledsoe seemed to be the better point guard on both ends of the floor, it might have been best for them to let Knight lead the second unit and give the starting shooting guard spot to the 19-year-old Devin Booker.

Breakout Year

After such a surprisingly successful rookie season for Devin Booker, what he needed to do next was continue to improve if he wanted to be any help for the Phoenix Suns, especially given their dreadfully bad 2015-16 record. Not content with the strides he made the past season, he worked hard on his game during the 2016 offseason to prove himself worthy of the starting spot and the designation as the team's franchise player.

During the offseason, he and coach Earl Watson met up in Los Angeles to train. They imported the services of retired NBA All-Star Baron Davis to help teach Booker some tricks of the trade. Spending about four hours in the gym with Davis, Booker learned certain misdirection moves and how to get the best possible shot he wanted off the dribble.[xiv] Of course, Devin had other workouts during the offseason as well.

Even though he had already achieved enough that he no longer needed to play in the Summer League, Devin Booker still participated in the NBA's annual July tournament as the de facto leader of the squad that the Phoenix Suns sent over to Las Vegas. For him, it was not because he wanted to dominate opponents that were just trying to get roster spots. Instead, it was still a part of his development as a player.

During the Summer League, Booker impressed people by showing how well he has improved as a ball-handler and playmaker. He was able to handle the ball well against tough defenses in traffic while maintaining his awareness as a playmaker that could find open teammates in any situation. Booker also showed that he could score well off the dribble by unveiling a quicker pull-up jumper.[xv]

Not known as a physical specimen, Booker proved that working out in the weight room pays off when he showed great balance as a finisher near the basket. He looked more physical and stronger than ever before when attacking and driving to the lane.[xv] Booker did not look like he was afraid of the contact and tried to finish strong instead of just pulling up near the basket for jumpers or floaters.

When asked what he did during the summer, Devin said that he focused on the overall aspect of his game. He worked on his jumper and shot while putting in the necessary heavy lifting inside the weight room. He placed a lot of emphasis on his diet and made sure he was eating right. Flexibility also played a significant role.[xv]

And while he may have been a big fish in a small pond during Summer League, Booker believed that he had to participate in the tournament to develop another aspect of his game that he could not work on in any training facility—leadership. Since he was being groomed as the Suns' shooting guard for the future, Devin also needed to grow as a leader. He needed to lead his team, but he could not do so on the Suns' normal roster because there were older and more experienced players taking the leadership roles. But during the Summer League, that leadership role was his for the taking.

Of course, Booker did not spend the entire summer playing for the Summer League squad because he also had to train together with and against some of the NBA's best stars as a member of USA Basketball's Select Team. He and some of the youngest and brightest stars of the league were set to train against the superstars and veterans of Team USA.[xvi]

It was a productive summer for Devin because he not only honed his leadership skills in the Summer League but also trained together with the big boys of USA Basketball. He also had the opportunity to be molded as a player that could one day represent his flag and country in international tournaments such as the Olympics or the FIBA Basketball World Cup as a member of Team USA.

After his summer duties for the Suns' Summer League team and USA Basketball, Booker spent most of his offseason in Phoenix training with the coaching staff, his teammates, and some guests from other teams. Despite being one of the youngest players on the roster, Booker was the guy who kept inviting players over for scrimmages. He was well beyond what his age and experience would normally show.

When the regular season started, Booker was the starting shooting guard while Brandon Knight was relegated to bench duties. It was a role that Booker would never relinquish because he kept improving and showing how good he was as a future star and as the Phoenix Suns' newest and brightest face of the franchise.

He made his 2016-17 debut against the Sacramento Kings on October 26, 2016. In that loss, Devin Booker had 18 points on 8 out of 12 shooting. He would then struggle in the next two games and it seemed like the opposing defenses were already preparing for him. Nevertheless, he and the Phoenix Suns made the right adjustments.

In just his fifth game of the season on November 4th, Booker helped the Phoenix Suns secure their second win by exploding for a new career high in points. Eclipsing his previous career high of 35 points, the 20-year-old went for 13 out of 22 from the field and 9 out of 9 from the free-throw line to score 38 points.

Two days later, Booker broke out once again to register a new career high in points. Shooting 13 out of 29 from the field and 10 out of 10 from the foul line, he scored 39 points in addition to the 7 assists he had in that loss to the Los Angeles Lakers. That performance made him the first Suns player in 28 years to score 38 or more points in consecutive games. The last player to do it was Tom Chambers almost three decades before.

Though it took time for him to explode for one of those high-scoring performances once again, Devin Booker remained a consistent scorer. He regularly scored in double digits for the struggling Phoenix Suns and was already becoming one of the top two players on that roster. He averaged 19.3 points on 43% shooting through his first 20 games of the regular season. Booker had four 30-point games at that juncture.

Booker continued to score in double digits in the next 17 games and would only miss the 10-point mark once. Most of his scoring performances were consistently on a 19-point average as the Suns' coaching staff continued to draw up plays exclusively to help the 20-year-old shooting guard get to his spot or get clean looks at the basket.

It would take until January 12, 2017, for Devin Booker to tie his career high. In that loss to the Dallas Mavericks, he made 14 of his 20 shots and 6 of his 7 three-pointers to score 39 points. Coming into the fourth quarter of that game, he only had 11 points. However, he was hot in the fourth and collected 28 points in that quarter alone. His 28-point performance in that quarter gave him the record for most points scored by a Suns player in a single quarter. It was a record held by

Stephon Marbury for almost a decade and a half before Booker broke it.

But Devin was not done. Two days later in Mexico City, he tied his career high once again. As the proud people of Mexico cheered on the player that has Mexican-American roots, Booker went for 12 out of 22 from the field and 12 out of 12 from the free-throw line to help the Suns beat the San Antonio Spurs. With that performance, he became the youngest player in league history to score 39 or more points in consecutive games.

As Devin Booker continued to improve his scoring prowess, he compiled a record that saw him going for 20 or more points in 16 consecutive games. He was the youngest player to do so. During that 16-game run from January 3rd to February 4th, Booker averaged 26.6 points, 2.8 rebounds, and 3.3 assists while shooting 46.8% from the field and 47.7% from the three-point line. And for the 14 games he played in January, he averaged 25.4 points.

The law of averages would catch up with Booker, however, as he could not sustain those high-scoring performances. Nevertheless, he took part as a starter for Team USA in the Rising Stars Challenge. He scored 17 points for Team USA, who lost that game to Team World. Booker would then take part in the Skills Challenge to showcase his improved ball-handling skills.

While Booker had a slow start to the second half of the season, he remedied that on March 11th when he went for 36 points on 12 out of

20 shooting from the field in a win over the Dallas Mavericks. A day later, he scored 28 points in addition to collecting 5 rebounds and 3 assists in a loss to the Portland Trail Blazers. But those performances were merely preludes to what was to come.

On March 24th in a game against the Boston Celtics, Booker exploded for a performance that only comes once in a generation even in the NBA. The 20-year-old, second-year player went on to make 21 of his 40 shots and 24 of his 26 free throws to compile 70 points in addition to the 8 rebounds, 6 assists, and 3 steals he had that night.

At age 20, no other player in league history has ever achieved such a feat. In fact, no 20-year-old player has even scored at least 60 in a single night. Michael Jordan could not do it. Kobe Bryant and LeBron James never scored at least 60 when they were 20. Even Wilt Chamberlain was already over 20 years old when he was putting up ridiculous scoring numbers. But Devin Booker scored 70 just five months after he turned 20 years old.

That 70-point performance was only the 11th time in league history that a player scored 70 or more points. The last player to do it was Kobe Bryant over 11 years before. Booker joined Bryant, David Robinson, Wilt Chamberlain, Elgin Baylor, and David Thompson as only the sixth player in NBA history to score 70 or more points.

That is a select company. And the best part about it for Devin was that he did it while he was only beginning to scratch the surface of his potential. All the other 70-point scorers accomplished it when they were in their respective primes.

Needless to say, Booker also broke the Suns' franchise record for most points scored in a single game. Tom Chambers once held that record with the 60 points he had in 1990. Booker also had 51 points in the second half alone. The record for most points in a half is still held by Wilt, but Booker's 51 points were still more than what Bryant put up in 2006.

Devi Booker also broke LeBron James' record for most points scored by a player under 21 years old. James had 56 when he was still 20. And finally, Booker's 70 points in that game were the most points anyone has ever scored against the Celtics. If you think about it, not even Wilt scored that many points against Boston. Booker was not even born the last time somebody scored 50 against the Celtics.

But how exactly did Booker achieve such a feat?

Coming into the game, the Suns probably had no chance against the East-leading Celtics. They also had no chance of getting into the playoffs even if they won all their remaining games. The factor of the matter was, Booker himself may have been shining, but the forecast was still dreary for the Suns, who were also missing two of their top three scorers. Because the team no longer had anything left to lose and they did not have anyone else to lean on, Devin Booker took matters into his own hands and tried to carry the team on his back.

Booker already had 19 points entering the second half. At that point, he had a decent chance of breaking into the 40-point mark for the first time in his career. The Celtics even inadvertently helped him achieve that feat by fouling the Suns several times during the third quarter. Because of that, Booker already had a new career high of 42 points after the third quarter.

Though Booker and the Suns were already down and had no reason to try to win that game, the young 20-year-old guard did not give up. He continued to seek the weakest points of the defense and attacked every matchup he saw. Before the halfway point of the quarter, he already had 50. And when there were less than two minutes left on the clock, he already had 61.

Of course, Devin Booker had some help.

Head coach Earl Watson called two timeouts and even asked his players to intentionally foul a Celtics player so that he could give more possessions to Devin. Watson wanted him to get 70 points and even asked his players to help him do something about it. Of course, Booker tried his best not only to score 70 points but also to give his team the win.

After he reached 64 points with a three-pointer in the last 80 seconds of the game, Devin Booker continued to attack the basket while the Celtics had no way to stop him except by fouling him. Booker's final six points came off the free-throw line as he finally reached the 70-

point mark with about 38 seconds left on the clock. He missed his next two shots as the Suns lost that game.

Devin Booker's performance that night was not selfish. Because the Suns lacked scorers and were still trying to win that game, Booker had to carry the scoring burden on his shoulders. He brought the Phoenix Suns back from a sure loss by consistently trying to score the ball. And when the 70-point mark was within reach, all he had to do was grab it while trying to give his team the win. It was like he was Kobe Bryant back in 2006 when the all-time great was trying to win a game against the Raptors while he scored 81 points.

Speaking of Bryant, Booker said that he got a bit of inspiration for his 70-point game from the Laker legend. Booker claimed that he had learned not to set a limit on his scoring when he watched one of Bryant's interviews back in the day. When Kobe told reporters that he never set a limit to how much he scored in a game, the idea got stuck in Devin's head. That was why Booker was trying to get the most points he could score in that game against the Celtics.[xvii] He was not specifically trying to get to 70, but he did not put a ceiling on how much he could score. All he did was try to stay aggressive all night long.

By staying aggressive and finding the weakest points on the defensive end during the entire game, Devin Booker broke his limits and looked a lot like Kobe Bryant. He was draining midrange jumpers, getting to the foul line, and destroying defenses on his own much, like Kobe did back in 2006. Like Bryant's performance, Booker's explosion was nothing short of incredible and historic.

After that 70-point game, Booker did not slow down and continued to score at least 21 points in his final seven games. He even scored 30 or more points thrice, as that 70-point performance lit an aggressive fire in the young shooting guard. Booker averaged 27.6 points and 6 assists in those final seven games.

After the conclusion of the regular season, the Phoenix Suns were lottery-bound once again with a 24-win campaign. Booker finished his second year with 22.1 points, 3.2 rebounds, and 3.4 assists. He led the team in scoring while shooting 42.3% from the floor and 36.3% from the three-point line as he elevated his game more quickly than anyone had expected. There was seemingly no ceiling to what Booker could achieve as he only continued to get better, stronger, and smarter with age and experience.

Rise to Stardom

Though Devin Booker had already concluded a breakout season, he was still far from being a complete product. Still turning 21 that season, the young guard was only beginning to scratch the surface of his potential. He had a lot of things to learn and work on before he could truly become a star. Thus, Devin used the 2017 offseason to work on becoming an even better player on both ends of the floor.

Even though he was still just 20 years old, Booker was now ineligible for the Summer League because he had already participated in it twice in the last two seasons. He wanted to play for the Summer League team once again, but Booker settled for training with the Phoenix Suns' young team during the summer. He ran scrimmages as well as team and individual drills with them as if he were trying to make the primary roster.[xviii]

The fact that Devin was training hard with the Summer League roster and making his presence felt, not only for the team but also for the people of Phoenix, was enough for the coaching staff to see how truly hardworking their budding young star truly was. And the fact that he was training with the Summer League squad for a third consecutive season meant that he did not care who he was training with or what level of basketball it was as long as he was taking steps to improve himself.

Booker was also planning to take on a bigger leadership role for the primary roster during the summer by leading team-wide workouts during the offseason instead of having the team go their individual and separate ways. While training individually might have helped the players, Booker wanted them to work together during the summer so that they could develop and grow together as one tight-knit unit. Devin believed that training with the entire team would not only help build chemistry from top to bottom but would also help him grow as a leader who would one day become the presence that stabilized the team.[xix]

Truth be told, it was just not feasible for every player on the Suns' roster to be present for team workouts during the offseason. Some players wanted to focus more on their individual workout routines while others preferred to decompress and spend time with their loved ones. In Devin Booker's case, he was talking about training with the young guys and incoming rookies that the Suns were hoping to grow with him.

The Phoenix Suns had a lot of young guys at that time. Marquese Chriss, Derrick Jones Jr., Dragan Bender, and Booker's former Kentucky teammate Tyler Ulis were just coming off their rookie seasons. The Suns also had 2017 NBA Draft fourth pick Josh Jackson coming in looking to make some noise in the NBA. And considering how young and inexperienced those players were at that time, Booker was sort of like a big brother to them, even though he was just coming into his third season as a 20-year-old rising star. In that sense, he needed to become the leader that helped those young players grow along with the team.

Devin also realized that mindset played a crucial role in helping the Phoenix Suns return to playoff contention. Even though he was already proving himself as a great individual player, Booker needed to become a winner to show that the Suns did not make a mistake when they made him the face of the franchise. Never setting a limit on his game, the young guard wanted to come into the next season with a mindset focused on becoming a better defender and a more vocal leader.[xix]

Coming into the next season, Devin Booker also had to grow in one other area of the game—playmaking. He had already developed well enough to become a scorer that could explode for 70 points in the blink of an eye. There were almost no doubts about his ability to put up points in a hurry. But because the NBA needed stars that could produce in other areas, Booker needed to become a better all-around player. As a guard set to become the unquestioned go-to guy of the Suns, the next logical step for him was to become a better playmaker.

In the NBA, it is important for designated pure scorers to develop their playmaking skills if they want to become stars. Kobe Bryant had to become a better passer because defenses always focused on him. Kevin Durant went from averaging 2.4 assists in his rookie season to averaging 5.5 assists in his MVP year in 2014. Even James Harden went from being a pure shooting guard to a point guard because he needed to become a playmaker to help his team win. In a sense, keeping defenses guessing whether you are going to score the ball or set your teammates up in an offensive play was a crucial aspect of what makes a superstar NBA player.

While Devin Booker was already showing flashes of brilliance as a playmaker since his rookie season, he needed to become an even better one, especially considering that the Phoenix Suns were going to draw up more plays for him and give him more possessions as the designated face of the franchise heading into the 2017-18 season. In a sense, he needed to become the team's pseudo point guard at the shooting guard position.

However, the problem was that the Suns had Eric Bledsoe locked in as the primary playmaker. This led the Suns to decide during the offseason that Devin Booker would share time with Bledsoe at the point guard spot. In a sense, Booker was going to be the primary playmaker whenever Bledsoe was on the bench. And giving the young shooting guard time at the point guard position was not only the next step for Booker in his evolution as a player, but was also the best move as the Suns inched closer to a time with the disgruntled Eric Bledsoe, who wanted to out of Phoenix.

The Phoenix Suns not only wanted Devin Booker to develop as a playmaker, but they also wanted to make him their temporary point guard when they did not have a starting point guard after finding a suitable trade destination for Eric Bledsoe. The Suns were trying to move toward a future with Devin Booker as their primary building block.

Unfortunately for Booker and the Suns, they were on the losing end of what was a humiliating blowout game on the team's opening night of the 2017-18 season. Booker finished with just 12 points in a 48-point loss against the Portland Trail Blazers on October 18, 2017. The loss was simply the byproduct of how young and inexperienced the team was.

Two days later, Booker nearly had the first triple-double game of his young career in a narrow loss to the Los Angeles Lakers. He finished that game with a great all-around stat line of 25 points, 11 rebounds, 8 assists, and 2 steals. He shot 9 out of 19 from the field and 4 out of 8 from the three-point line in that terrific individual performance.

It would take a few games for Booker to go on another of his explosive scoring barrages. On October 28th, his sixth game of the season, the third-year shooting guard went for 36 points, 6 rebounds, and 6 assists in a loss to the Portland Trail Blazers. With that game, he became third all-time in most 30-point games before the age of 21. It was just two days before he turned 21 years old.

Then, just a day after he turned 21 years old, Booker went for 32 points, 7 rebounds, and 4 assists in a win over the Brooklyn Nets. Finally, rounding up his third 30-point performance in a span of four games, he would go for 34 points on 10 out of 19 shooting from the floor in a loss to the New York Knicks on November 3rd.

Three days later, Devin Booker scored 18 in a loss to the Nets to become the fourth-youngest player in NBA history to reach 3,000 career points. Only LeBron James, Kevin Durant, and Carmelo Anthony were younger than Booker when they reached 3,000 career points. Devin Booker was even younger than Kobe Bryant when the latter got to that mark.

On November 11th, Devin Booker went for a new season high of 35 points when he shot 13 out of 22 from the field in a win over the Minnesota Timberwolves. He also finished with nine rebounds and six assists in that game. Then, just two days later, he eclipsed that mark by going for a new season high of 36 points on a 14 out of 27 shooting clip from the field.

Then, in a loss to the Houston Rockets on November 16th, Booker did his best James Harden impression by going for his second double-double performance of the season with 18 points and 10 assists. He followed that up a night later by going for 33 points on 13 out of 27 shooting from the field in a win over the Los Angeles Lakers.

Still not done, Devin Booker outdid himself by going for a new season high in points on December 2nd. In that loss to the Boston Celtics, he proved his mastery over his opponent's defense by following up his 70-point performance with 38 massive points on 16 out of 29 shooting. While the Celtics had learned to adjust to prevent Booker from going for another outburst, Booker proved that he was good enough to score well against one of the best defensive teams in the league that season.

After that season-high performance against the Celtics, Booker would explode once more for a hot scoring night. In a win over the Philadelphia 76ers, he went for 46 points and 8 rebounds while shooting 17 out of 32 from the floor and 5 out of 8 from the three-point line. That was only the second time that Booker scored 40 or more points in a single game.

But on December 6th, the Phoenix Suns announced that Devin Booker would be out for a few weeks because of an injury he sustained in a game against the Toronto Raptors the night before. He had 19 points and 8 assists that night, but it was evident that he was nursing an injury after shooting just 4 out of 15 from the field in the 39 minutes he played.

Booker missed nine consecutive games, and the Suns would only win three of those outings. But when he came back, it seemed as if he did not lose his step. Showing that his injury did not bother him, Booker went for 32 points, 5 rebounds, and 6 assists while shooting 9 out of 21 from the floor in his return game for the Phoenix Suns. He then went on to score 30 or more points in two of the next three games, averaging 31 points, 4.5 rebounds, and 5.5 assists in the first four games since his return from the injury.

On January 16, 2018, Booker would have another high-scoring game when he exploded for 43 points to go along with 6 rebounds and 8 assists in a loss to the Portland Trail Blazers. He shot 14 out of 29 from the field and 10 out of 10 from the free-throw line in that game. And proving that he was still hot from the floor, he would go for 30 just three days later in a win over the Denver Nuggets.

Devin Booker would go for only his third double-double performance of the season on January 28th when the Phoenix Suns lost to the Houston Rockets. In that game, he went for 31 points and 10 assists as he arguably outplayed James Harden on both ends of the floor. However, he would then miss a few games because of a hip injury.

When All-Star Weekend came, Booker did not make the cut. It was understandable because of how poorly the Suns were performing, his time missed due to injury, and also how deep the talent pool among guards was in the Western Conference. While Booker was having a better season that year, it was hard to choose him as an All-Star over guards such as Stephen Curry, Russell Westbrook, James Harden, Damian Lillard, and Klay Thompson.

However, Devin Booker did have his own All-Star Weekend moment. Proving that he was already one of the best shooters in the world, he defeated an all-time great shooter in Klay Thompson during the Three-Point Contest. In doing so, he set a new record of 28 points in the final round. That win helped show how great of a marksman Booker had become.

Using the excitement of his All-Star Weekend success to his advantage, Devin had a scorching-hot start to the second half of the season. On February 24th, he went for 30 points in a loss to the Blazers. After that, he went for arguably his best performance of the season with 40 points, 10 rebounds, and 7 assists in a loss to the New Orleans Pelicans. He followed that up with 34 points and 6 rebounds in a win over the Memphis Grizzlies on February 28th. Finally, he went for 39 points against the Oklahoma City Thunder on March 2nd.

After scoring 30 or more points for four straight games, Booker became the first Phoenix Suns player since 2004 to score at least 30 points in four consecutive outings. The last one to do it was Amar'e Stoudemire. During that run, Booker was averaging 36 points, 8 rebounds, and 5 assists. And in the five games following the All-Star Weekend, he averaged 34 points.

Devin Booker also completed a personal milestone with that 39-point performance against the Thunder. In that game, he reached 4,000 career points to become the third-youngest player in league history to reach that mark. Only LeBron James and Kevin Durant were younger than Booker when they achieved that career milestone. That achievement placed him in select company as one of the best young scorers in NBA history.

At 21 years old, Devin was already putting up points and scoring at a pace that not even seasoned NBA veterans could. He was only as old as some juniors and seniors in college and yet he was already outplaying some of the best basketball players in the world. Nobody thought that the 18-year-old kid coming out of Kentucky after just one season was capable of such a feat. And if some people thought he could do it, they would still not believe that he could achieve such heights in just his third season in the league and at 21 years old.

To put it in perspective, Carmelo Anthony was already a designated 20-point scorer when he came out of college and Kobe Bryant was barely 18 years old when he came out of high school. Meanwhile, Devin Booker had a slow start to his rookie season and was about a year older than Kobe when the latter was an NBA rookie. However, he still outpaced both Anthony and Bryant on his way to 4,000 career points. That goes to show how fast Booker was developing as an individual player.

Unfortunately for Booker, he would not have more opportunities to add onto his career scoring total that season. He was ruled out of the Phoenix Suns' final 12 games of the season because of a right hand injury he sustained a few games after hitting the 4,000-point mark. In those final 12 games, the Phoenix Suns only won two outings and were well on their way to the lottery yet again.

After his third season in the league, Devin Booker averaged 24.9 points, 4.5 rebounds, 4.7 assists, and 0.9 steals. He also shot 43.2% from the floor, 38.3% from the three-point line, and 87.8% from the foul stripe. Given those figures, it was evident that he had increased his statistics across the board. That meant that all the hard work he had put in during the offseason had indeed paid off, though he was still missing the playoff appearance that would have helped to establish him as one of the best young players in the NBA.

But to once again put his accomplishments into perspective, Devin Booker finished the season with a true shooting percentage of 56.1%. What makes that great? Well, only Michael Jordan and LeBron James have ever posted a similar true shooting percentage at the age of 21 while averaging at least 24 points, 4.5 assists, and 4.5 rebounds.[xx] Nobody else that young has been as efficient as Devin Booker was as a scorer. And he was doing that even though he was not as athletic as

Jordan and James were when they were 21. The scary part is that he would only get better.

The Max Player, Phoenix's New Face of the Franchise

If there was a consolation to the Phoenix Suns' dreadfully bad 2017-18 season, it was that they performed so poorly that the ping-pong balls bounced their way during the NBA's annual draft lottery. They would win the first overall in the 2018 NBA Draft. And they would exercise this right by drafting physically imposing and gracefully skillful center Deandre Ayton out of Arizona.

With Ayton in the mix, the Phoenix Suns had a chance to speed up their rebuilding process, since they already had two talented players in Deandre Ayton and Josh Jackson helping Devin Booker bring the franchise back to relevance. Josh Jackson was going to be the perimeter defensive force taking a lot of burden off Booker's shoulders because the latter would not be forced to defend the other team's best perimeter player. Meanwhile, Ayton was going to be their inside presence on both ends of the floor. It was like he was going to be the Shaq (or at least the Bynum or Gasol) to Booker's Kobe.

Because the Suns were trusting that Booker was going to lead them back to their glory days as the franchise's best player, they offered him a five-year max contract extension worth $158 million. This meant that the franchise did indeed believe in what he could do for them. It also meant that Booker was going to be staying with Phoenix for at least five more seasons barring any trades involving his contract.

But what did the max contract mean for him? It meant that Booker now had to put in more effort to prove that he was worth the franchise's trust. As good as he was that last season, and as impressive as his statistics were, he was still lacking in some areas that max contract players were expected to excel at.

For starters, he needed to work on becoming a better defender. On the offensive end, it was hard to question what he was capable of because he is a player that can score in the three main areas of scoring: off the drive, off the dribble, and off the catch. And he does well in those three areas as shown by his true shooting percentage.

However, he still had not proven himself as a good defender that could lock opposing players up. While Booker showed improvements in that area, especially when playing one-on-one in isolation situations, he still had trouble covering players in certain situations, such as the pick-and-roll. Nevertheless, one could argue that he was already doing his best with the teammates he had helping him out on the defensive end.

This made the 2018-19 season crucial for Booker because now the entire team would see what he is capable of with quality players helping him out. As mentioned, Josh Jackson would be there to help him cover the best perimeter players on the defensive end while

Deandre Ayton would allow him and the other defenders to feel at ease knowing that there was a huge center guarding the basket.

Mikal Bridges, the team's other rookie draft pick in 2018, could also be the X-factor Devin Booker needed. Bridges showed in his three seasons at Villanova that he was a capable three-point shooter and finisher at the basket. He could also defend well. Booker did not even have a teammate that could reliably shoot, finish, and defend well during the previous season, but he still put up good assist numbers for a shooting guard. As good as T.J. Warren and Josh Jackson were for the Suns in the previous season, they were not floor spacers that could produce well from the outside.

With Mikal Bridges waiting in the wings or in the corner for passes, and with Ayton as the primary pick-and-roll/pop option, Booker was primed for the best passing season of his young career. It was a make-or-break season for him because this time, nobody could make excuses about why he was not winning enough games. He now had quality players helping him out on both ends of the floor.

Although it was still too early to say that the Phoenix Suns would make the playoffs because of how tough the competition is in the Western Conference, the best that anyone could expect out of Booker and his team was that they would come out better than ever. And if they somehow stayed stagnant or even plummeted lower than they were, maybe Booker was not worth that max contract after all. But given what Devin has done in the last three seasons with what little help he had, it might be farfetched to think that he and the Suns would stagnate.

However, Devin Booker's stint as Phoenix's designated max contract franchise player would not start out so well. Just five weeks before the start of the 2018-19 regular season, the 21-year-old guard was diagnosed with a broken right hand. Still, Booker managed to recover in time for the start of the season and he was ready to help the Suns in what was another campaign that could possibly push the team forward.

In his first game during the 2018-19 season, Booker had 35 points and 7 assists in a win over the Dallas Mavericks on October 17, 2018. However, the Suns went on to have a dismal record early in the season, having won only 4 of their first 29 games. Booker was still playing well, however. He went for 30 or more points regularly during that stretch but it was beginning to look like the Suns just did not have the experience or the personnel that allowed them to compete against some of the best teams in the league. The changes they had made to the roster were not yet paying off. It also did not help that Booker missed a few games due to minor injuries.

Despite the fact that he was not going to win a lot of games that season, Booker still showed his potential as one of the best up-and-coming guards in the league. He posted 38 points in a win over the New York Knicks on December 17th. Then, a few days later, he recorded 33 points and 14 assists in a narrow loss to the Washington Wizards. It was clear that he was not only developing as a scorer but had also become a capable playmaker that utilized his ability to read offenses and understand teammate tendencies.

Then again, the losing continued for the Suns. Phoenix lost 17 straight games from January 15th to February 23, 2019. While the budding star performed well in those games, the rest of the Suns were still trying to figure things out on both ends of the floor. Despite the losses, he still continued to climb the ladder of great young scorers. On January 24, 2019, Booker became the fifth youngest player in NBA history to reach 5,000 career points, behind LeBron James, Kevin Durant, Carmelo Anthony, and Dwight Howard.[xxi]

With the season already a bust for the entire Phoenix Suns team, Booker failed to make it to the All-Star Game largely because his squad was not in the best position to compete. On top of that, there were far too many stellar guards for Booker to compete against in the Western Conference, and they all had notably better teams. In that regard, Booker still needed to wait before he could make the All-Star team.

That was despite the fact that he was putting up All-Star numbers at that time. He had 41 points in a win over the Knicks on March 6th and 40 points and 13 assists in a win over the New Orleans Pelicans on March 16th. But the most impressive part of his season was the three-game stretch he had from March 25th to the 30th, wherein he averaged 52.3 points. He had 59 points on the Utah Jazz, 50 points against the Wizards, and 48 points and 11 assists against the Grizzlies. Nevertheless, all of those games were losses.

In what was his best statistical season at that point in his career, Devin Booker averaged 26.6 points and 6.8 assists. However, his Phoenix Suns finished with a grim record of just 19 wins and 63 losses. That meant that this team still had a lot of work left to do before it would be ready to finally make some noise in the tough Western Conference.

The Rising Suns

There were a lot of problems that led to the bad season that the Suns had during the 2018-19 campaign. Of course, coaching was one of their weaknesses, and that was remedied when the team brought in a tried and tested coach in Monty Williams, who was able to succeed as a coach well enough in the teams that he handled in the past. They may have already added some key support for Booker in Jackson and Ayton, but the fact remained that the team just did not have a point guard.

The point guard rotation for the Suns during the 2018-19 season was bad, as they had to play young and unproven guards like Elie Okobo and De'Anthony Melton at the starting point guard slot. But the worst part was that the NBA was now a point guard-oriented league that utilized stellar point guards as the points of attack for any offense. Not having a capable point guard hurt the Suns on both offense and defense. In fact, Booker had had to shoulder the playmaking load a season ago. But the good thing was that the Suns brought in Ricky

Rubio, who may not have been the best point guard as far as scoring was concerned but he was always a great playmaker and a capable defender.

Having a capable coach and a true point guard changed a lot of things for the Suns heading into the 2019-20 season. But the team's future still hinged on whether or not Devin Booker could rise together with the other Suns as the undoubted franchise player and a true star. He was only 23 years old but was already in his fifth season in the league. And this was the best time for him to prove any of his doubters wrong and become an All-Star for the first time in his career.

Booker did indeed rise to the occasion and went on to perform like a true star during the 2019-20 season, all while the rest of the Suns ascended with him. In a win over the Philadelphia 76ers on November 4th, Booker finished with an incredibly efficient performance of 40 points on just 15 out of 19 from the field. Then, in a win over the Minnesota Timberwolves on November 23rd, he finished with 35 points, 12 rebounds, and 9 assists in what was nearly a triple-double effort for the rising star. Then, against the Pelicans on December 5th, he had a new season high of 44 points together with 8 rebounds and 9 assists.

The best part was that the Suns, although far from contending for a championship in the West, were no longer doormats that the other teams could expect a win from. They were finally competing well and had miraculously come a long way for a team that did not look like it had any chance of becoming a future playoff contender just a year ago. The critical changes made during the 2019 offseason worked wonders for the team.

Booker, of course, continued to showcase why he was a star in the league at that point in his career. Often seen as a merely average young talent that just did not have the ability to get over the hump and become a great player on a team that could compete, he rose to the occasion and delivered whenever he was needed most. After the Suns struggled with seven straight losses, Booker answered back by delivering seven straight games of scoring 30 or more points. He averaged 34.7 points and 6.9 assists while shooting nearly 55% from the field in those seven games. The highlight was when he had 40 points in a loss to the Memphis Grizzlies on January 5, 2020.

In fact, Booker was so good during the month of January 2020 that he was seemingly proving himself as a legitimate case for one of the backcourt spots for the All-Star team in a Western Conference that was deep in the guard rotation. During that month, he averaged 31.3 points while shooting 52.2% from the field. He had nine games of scoring 30 or more points. Aside from that 40-point output, one of his highlights included a win over the Boston Celtics, wherein he finished with 39 points, 10 rebounds, and 9 assists.

But while Booker's January was great in terms of his performances on the court, he had to endure the pain of the loss of one of his childhood idols. Kobe Bryant died in a helicopter accident on January 26, 2020.

A lot of the players that played during that era looked up to Kobe. Bryant was an icon that they loved watching when they were young. Of course, Booker was one of those young players.

Devin idolized the Black Mamba when he was still just a young boy. In fact, he patterned a large part of his game after Kobe's own style. That was why, despite the fact that Booker was seen as a knockdown outside shooter, he ended up becoming a midrange specialist—that was due to Kobe's effect on his game. News of the legendary icon's tragic death was devastating to him.

"It's been a lot of what I do, man, mentality wise, approach wise everything, before I even knew him personally, he had shaped my life. My basketball career. My approach to everything."

"The biggest thing for me was earning his respect," Booker said. "To even be the guy in the room after we play them that he wanted to talk to or share advice with. Then our relationship had grown from there. Just figuring out what type of person he was outside of the Mamba mentality. How he raised his daughters and how much of a family man he was something that was just incredible."[xxii]

Like Bryant, Booker had entered the league at a younger age than the norm and had a lot of potential at that early age due to how refined his game already was. Of course, Kobe was more of a spectacular athlete during his younger years but he already showed how dangerous he could be with his fundamentals and footwork. Booker specifically patterned the fundamental aspect of his game after the older version of Bryant, who relied more on his refined midrange jumper and ability to create space with his footwork. But while they were very similar in a lot of different on-court aspects, Booker worked hard to earn the respect of the late great Kobe Bryant, who was always known for his competitive edge and ability to work harder than everyone else.

His hard work finally paid off because Devin Booker, for the first time in his career, was an All-Star. But he was almost snubbed out of the midseason classic. He was not even selected as part of the initial lineup of reserves due to how deep the West was. That was not even counting Stephen Curry, who was injured throughout the season. But because Damian Lillard could not make it to the All-Star Game due to an injury, Booker was finally given the respect he rightfully deserved when he became a true All-Star at the tender age of 23.

More than a month after Kobe's death, Devin Booker got his first tattoo, which was his own way of honoring his fallen idol. Back when he was still just a rookie in 2016, which was Kobe's final year in the league, Booker asked Bryant to sign his sneakers after a game against him. The words that the Black Mamba wrote on his sneakers were "Be legendary," a phrase that Booker ultimately lived by. As such, he immortalized these words on his skin when he got tattoos that say "Be legendary." And the start of what could be a legendary career was marked by his first All-Star appearance in 2020.

Shortly after the 2020 All-Star Game, the world of professional sports came to a screeching halt due to the outbreak of COVID-19, which had become a deadly pandemic. After Rudy Gobert became the first player in the NBA to get diagnosed with the virus, the league had to suspend its operations, just like how most of the entire world was forced to quarantine. The NBA officially suspended the 2019-20 season on March 11, 2020, as it took nearly five months for the league to resume the regular season.

Eventually, the NBA stakeholders, which include the team owners, the league office, and the Players Association, decided to resume the season. The agreement was that they were going to conclude the season in Disney World in Orlando, Florida, where a "bubble" would be set up so that the players and coaches would be isolated in a single area.

Only the top eight teams of both conferences and the teams that were within eight wins away from the eighth spot of their respective conferences were allowed to go to the Orlando Bubble. Luckily for the Phoenix Suns, they qualified to make it to the Orlando, where they were going to play eight games to determine whether or not they would qualify for the playoffs.

When the 2019-2020 season resumed in the final days of July 2020, the Suns showed a glimpse of what the future could be for the team. They surprised a lot of people with the way they performed in the Bubble. It might have been a product of rust on the part of the other teams, or it could have also been a product of the different environment that the players were playing in. But the fact that the

Suns were playing out of their minds was one of the best stories of the Orlando Bubble.

Booker, of course, was one of the main catalysts of that surprising Bubble performance for the Phoenix Suns. He was a consistent force for Phoenix throughout those eight games, as he never scored under 20 points the entire time he was there. Booker even racked up three straight games of scoring 35 points to give his team a chance to make the Bubble playoffs.

During the eight-game stretch in Orlando, Devin Booker averaged 30.5 points, 4.9 rebounds, and 6 assists while shooting an efficient clip of 50.3% from the field. The most impressive part was that Phoenix went 8-0 in the Bubble. Believe it or not, the Suns were the only team that did not lose a single game in the Bubble! But because other teams did enough to finish with a better record overall, the Suns *still* did not qualify for the playoffs.

Even so, Devin Booker was outstanding. He averaged 26.6 points, 4.2 rebounds, and 6.5 assists while shooting around 49% from the field during the 2019-20 season. His team finished with a record of 34-39, which was the best that the Suns have had in a very long time. And it was that undefeated run in the Bubble that gave this team a lot of hope. It was clear that the sun was rising in Phoenix.

Making the Playoffs, Finals Appearance

As impressive as the 8-0 run in the Bubble was for the Phoenix Suns, the puzzle was yet to be completed. They needed one more piece that could help the team get over the hump and finally return to the playoffs for the first time in over a decade. That was when Kelly Oubre Jr., Ricky Rubio, Ty Jerome, Jalen Lecque, and a 2022 protected first-round pick were traded to the Oklahoma City Thunder for the services of Chris Paul.

While Paul may have already been an older man in the NBA at that point in his career, he had compiled a resume that made him one of the greatest pure point guards the league has ever seen. He was a consistent winner that led his teams to playoff appearances due to his playmaking, passing, and timely scoring. But it was his leadership that coaches loved about him most. Paul always had a way of pushing his teammates to become better versions of themselves. One case in point was the 2019-2020 Oklahoma City Thunder team that was not expected to make the playoffs because the young squad was in the middle of a rebuild. However, Chris Paul's competitive spirit and leadership allowed the team to make the postseason and push the Houston Rockets to seven games during the first round of the playoffs in the Orlando Bubble.

There was no question that Paul was already old in basketball years. But the way he took care of his body and the fact that his game was more reliant on his skills and IQ allowed him to stay relevant in the

NBA even as a new crop of young point guards was entering the league. And the fact that Paul was a veteran leader that has seen his fair share of wars on the court was the reason why he was the missing piece that the Suns needed to finally end their playoff drought.

While Ricky Rubio was a great player for Phoenix last season because he gave the team a true point guard, Chris Paul was an upgrade due to his offense and leadership. Both of them knew how to pass the ball at exceptional levels but Paul's offense made him a bigger threat to opposing teams because he was the master of the elbow midrange jumper and was still capable of taking the ball all the way to the basket. Having Paul around meant that Booker's playmaking duties would be decreased. It also meant that he could now focus on what he did best—scoring.

Of course, Booker and his fellow young teammates were steadily improving as well. Mikal Bridges was improving as a perimeter defender and was always available whenever he was needed. Cam Johnson was a revelation last season and proved to be a capable scoring threat as well. Meanwhile, Deandre Ayton was set to have an efficient season because he could now simply wait in the paint for lob passes from both Paul and Booker.

But another key ingredient was Monty Williams and his coaching philosophy. Under him, the Suns were much more competitive on both ends of the floor. It was his defensive schemes that truly allowed Phoenix to rise up and become a threat to the league. Their offense was always going to be there because of the offensive brilliance of Paul and Booker. But the entire team needed to step up on the defensive end as well. And they did.

In what was a shortened 72-game season that began in December of 2020, Booker and the Suns carried the momentum from the Bubble to the 2020-21 season as they won five of their first six games to start the season. Booker did not even have to explode for high-scoring performances during that stretch because the Suns were winning through the solid all-around contributions of everyone on the roster.

The young All-Star missed a few games during the early part of the season but came back stronger and had a lot of explosive performances in February, all while leading the Suns to six straight wins and a 12-3 record. During that stretch, he had 36 points on February 8th in a win over the Cleveland Cavaliers. He tied that output five days later in a win over the Philadelphia 76ers. Then, on February 28th, Booker went for a new season high of 43 points in a win over the Minnesota Timberwolves.

Booker led the Suns once more to a winning streak during the latter portion of the season. Phoenix won seven straight games from March 28th to April 7th. In the final four games of that streak, he scored at least 32 points consecutively. It was on March 31st that he had a new season-high 45 points in a win over the Chicago Bulls.

As such, Booker was clearly established as an All-Star that was selected once more as an injury replacement. However, because of a knee injury, he had to sit the All-Star Game out that season. Still, he and Paul became the first Suns duo to make it to the All-Star Game for the first time since 2010 when Steve Nash and Amar'e Stoudemire were still the dangerous pick-and-roll threat that they were.

The stellar play and leadership of Paul allowed Phoenix to rise up as a legitimate threat in the Western Conference that season. Things were also easier for Booker, who continued to rack up personal accomplishments during that campaign. He passed Dan Majerle for tenth place among the Suns' all-time leading scorers. It was also during that season that he reached 8,000 career points and 700 career three-pointers.

Because the Suns had more weapons that season and were relying on the playmaking of CP3, Booker did not have the same stats he did in the last two seasons. Still, he averaged 25.6 points, 4.2 rebounds, and 4.3 assists. He helped the Phoenix Suns secure the second seed in the Western Conference. Phoenix ended the season with a record of 51-21, which was only one win away from the first-seeded Utah Jazz.

The second-seeded Phoenix Suns had made the playoffs for the first time since 2010 thanks to the renewed all-around effort from everyone on the team. While Booker and Paul were showing glimpses of what could have happened had Chris Paul been allowed to play with Kobe Bryant more than a decade ago, the other players on the team stepped up as well to give the fans something to look forward to.

After six seasons in the NBA, Devin Booker finally made it to the playoffs for the first time in his career. It was fitting that the first team that he faced in his playoff debut was the team that his childhood idol had played for his entire life. The Suns were set to face the seventh-seeded Los Angeles Lakers in the first round of the 2021 playoffs. Of course, this was a daunting test for the Suns because the Lakers were the defending champions.

Even though the Suns were the higher-seeded team in this matchup, they were still seen as the underdogs by some people because they lacked playoff experience and were coming in against the defending champions. Nevertheless, Booker showed what he could do in his first playoff game when he played 45 minutes to deliver 34 points in his debut in Game 1.

The Lakers, however, showed their championship experience in the next two games to put pressure on the Suns. But Los Angeles lost its mojo throughout the rest of the playoffs. After the Suns won Game 4 by 8 points, they dictated the tempo of the series by winning Game 5 to go up 3-2 in the series. Devin Booker had 30 points in that outing. However, his best playoff game was in Game 6 in Los Angeles. Booker played all but two minutes of that game to deliver one of his greatest playoff performances as he went for 47 points and 11 rebounds. There would be no Game 7.

Winning that series against the Lakers meant that the Suns dethroned the defending champions and they were going to be champions themselves. And considering that Phoenix defeated the team that was still one of the favorites to come out of the West, the Suns were now heavy favorites to represent the conference in the NBA Finals.

But the Suns needed to make sure that they had what it took to defeat their next two opponents to get to the finals. After all, the last time the Suns were in the finals was in 1993 when Charles Barkley was still the best player in the franchise. And it is worth mentioning that the Suns organization is one of the teams that are yet to win an NBA championship.

In the second round, the Denver Nuggets were looking to give the Phoenix Suns a tough fight. After all, the Nuggets went all the way to the Western Conference Finals during the Orlando Bubble. On top of that, Nikola Jokic was playing out of his mind as the favorite to win the NBA MVP that season. That meant that the Suns had a lot on their plate because of the presence of Jokic, who was already one of the best players in the league.

While Booker was a flamethrower that scored a lot of points during the first round against the Lakers, he was more of a facilitator and timely scorer in the second round against the Nuggets. The Suns utilized a fantastic all-around onslaught from their starters to win Game 1 by double digits. Booker, Paul, Ayton, and Bridges all scored 20 or more points in that win.

In Game 2, Booker and the Suns used another balanced offensive attack to defeat the Nuggets in a blowout game. He finished with 18 points and 10 rebounds, all while Chris Paul had 17 points and 15 assists. Four other players scored in double digits in that balanced effort from the Suns. But while he was a bit mellow during the first two games of the series, Booker stamped his name all over Game 3 to deliver 28 points and put the Suns in a position that all but guaranteed that they would win the series.

The inevitable happened in Game 4 when the Phoenix Suns swept the series and defeated the Denver Nuggets in the second round. Devin Booker paced the Suns for 34 points. But it was Chris Paul who led them to the Western Conference Finals by going for 37 points on an efficient 73.7% shooting clip.

That series win over the Denver Nuggets catapulted the Phoenix Suns to the Western Conference Finals for the first time since 2010, which was also the last time they saw the playoffs. The WCF in 2021 was a meeting between teams that do not always get that deep in the playoffs. The Suns were up against the Clippers in that game. In that regard, the NBA was going to see a fresh face in the finals.

While the Clippers were shorthanded because they did not have Kawhi Leonard, who was their best player, they fought hard enough in the playoffs to get as far as they did. Paul George was shedding the label of him being a playoff choker. Meanwhile, Reggie Jackson was playing the best basketball of his life at that point in his career.

But while the Clippers were fighting well enough despite being shorthanded, they were not ready for Booker's initial onslaught. In what was his finest playoff performance from an all-around standpoint, he went for 40 points, 13 rebounds, and 11 assists in that Game 1 win over the Clippers. This was a tough matchup, but things only got tougher in Game 2. In what was one of the greatest alley-oop plays of all time, the Suns went for an inbound alley-oop that allowed Deandre Ayton to flush the ball and give Phoenix the win.

The Suns dropped Game 3 in Los Angeles as the Clippers made the series more competitive. But another hard-fought outing in Game 4 gave the Suns a 3-1 lead that was almost impossible for any opposing team to return from. Of course, the Clippers tried hard in Game 5. But Booker scored 22 in what was a strong 27-point win for the Phoenix Suns in Game 6.

In his first appearance in the playoffs, Devin Booker was now on his way to his first NBA Finals. The stars were now seemingly aligned for the Suns. They had all the opportunity in the world to put a stamp on what was a surprising season for a team that was historically known to struggle to win games in the regular season and could not make a deep run in the playoffs. But Booker proved himself a true franchise player when he led his team all the way to the finals in his first postseason.

Standing in the way of the Phoenix Suns in the finals were the Milwaukee Bucks, another tough team with an MVP-caliber player in Giannis Antetokounmpo, who was already known as the most dominant player in the league and was quite arguably the best basketball player in the world at that time. Although Giannis was nursing a knee injury heading into the finals, the duo of Khris Middleton and Jrue Holiday were more than ready to help him at any given moment.

During the first two games of the finals, however, the Suns carried the momentum of their historic season to give the Bucks a scare. They won those first two games by double digits because everyone on that team stepped up and delivered when they were asked to do so. Booker delivered 27 points in   Game 1 before going for 31 points in Game 2. And the Suns were only two wins away from the franchise's first-ever championship.

But the Milwaukee Bucks put on their hardhats in the next four games to surprise the Phoenix Suns. More importantly, the Bucks had Giannis, who had one of the greatest finals series of all time. Despite the fact that Phoenix had great perimeter defenders like Miles Bridges, Jae Crowder, and Torrey Craig, none of them could match up well with Antetokounmpo due to his strength. Ayton had the size to match Giannis in the paint but he just was not nimble enough for the two-time MVP. Simply put, Giannis was too much of a beast and a matchup nightmare for the Suns to stop. And the rest of the Bucks followed their leader.

Milwaukee won Game 3 to get within one win away from tying the series. Booker, however, was not willing to give Game 4 away because he delivered 42 big points in that performance for the Suns.

The Bucks, however, were up two points in the final minute of the game in Game 4. Booker played decoy in the next play because he knew that the defense would focus on him. However, he threw a lob pass to Ayton, who would have flushed that down 99% of the time. But this time it was Giannis who was waiting to recover in the paint just in time to deliver a game-saving block that ultimately became the play of the finals. As such, the Milwaukee Bucks survived Booker's 42-point output and knotted the series up.

With the series tied two games apiece and momentum now swinging toward Milwaukee, the Suns needed to win Game 5 to regain the psychological advantage over the Bucks heading into Game 6. This was the closest game of the series because no one was willing to give an inch. Of course, the result of the game had to be decided by another memorable play. Sadly, the play did not favor the Suns.

The Bucks were up a solitary point with 29 seconds left, as Booker brought the ball up the floor after a rebound. With 40 points under his name, he was in the best position to give the team a basket in that tough situation for the Suns. He took the ball near the paint but was met with multiple defenders. That was when Jrue Holiday stripped the ball from him and ran away with it before throwing a lob pass for Giannis for the most iconic dunk of the series.

As such, 40 points from Booker were not enough to give the Suns the series lead once more as their backs were up against the wall heading into Game 6 in Milwaukee. He may have been only the third player in finals history to record 40 or more points in back-to-back games, but he needed help from his teammates on both ends of the floor if he wanted to stay alive in the finals.

Winning Game 6 would have placed the Suns in a good position to win Game 7 because they had homecourt advantage. As such, the focus was to make sure that they stayed alive long enough to take the finals back home in Phoenix. But Giannis Antetokounmpo dominated once more as he was incredibly aggressive all game long. No defensive strategy was enough to slow down the Greek Freak, who stamped his name all over Game 6 to deliver 50 huge points. Booker also had one of his worst shooting performances all series long because he was limited to 19 points on 8 out of 22 from the floor.

As such, the Bucks returned from the dead by winning four games in a row after the Suns took the first two games of the finals. Milwaukee raised the championship trophy at the expense of Phoenix in what was Devin Booker's first-ever finals appearance. Antetokounmpo had one of the greatest finals performances at the expense of a rising star in the form of Booker. Nevertheless, as Chris Paul said, that finals appearance was so addictive that it only made them want to return to the championship picture once more. And it was this experience in the finals that made the Suns desperate to make a return trip in the future.

Continued Excellence

Entering the 2021-22 season, the Phoenix Suns were favorites to return to the finals because they had already proven themselves capable enough to defeat any challenger in the Western Conference. Of course, there were also other teams rising in the West, while some of the veteran teams were still playing well. It remained a very tough conference to compete in. But the Suns kept their roster intact in an attempt to make a return trip to the championship round, where they could have a chance to win it all again.

While the Suns started the season 1-3 after a short finals hangover, they started clicking late in October of 2021 and were unstoppable during the early part of the 2021-22 season. The Suns started winning and winning and winning until it was clear that they were not going to lose any time soon. It came to a point where they won 18 straight games and were undefeated with a 16-0 record in November. Devin Booker called this amazing stretch of games "No Loss November," as it was clear that the Suns were the team to beat in the West.

Booker was not even playing out of his mind during that streak of wins for Phoenix because it was more of an all-around team effort for the Suns. Still, he was the catalyst for that streak because the wins halted when he was out for seven straight games due to a minor injury. But Booker came back strong and delivered win after win after win for Phoenix in what was clearly one of the best seasons a team could ever hope for.

From January 11th to February 24th of 2022, Devin Booker led his team to a 19-1 record in the 20 games that the Suns played during that span. This included 11 straight wins for the Phoenix Suns, and Devin

Booker was at his best in that winning streak. After going for 35 and 30 points in wins over Indiana and Detroit, he had a new season high of 48 points in a win over the San Antonio Spurs on January 17th. He outdid himself on January 26th when he delivered 43 points and 12 rebounds in a win over the Utah Jazz.

Of course, performances like those proved that Booker was a clear All-Star that no longer had to take someone's spot due to injury. He was chosen as a reserve for the 2022 All-Star Game. As such, there was no doubt that he was an elite player that had the stats and the wins that proved his superiority over a lot of the other talented guards out in the West.

The Suns were the clear favorites in the West due to their record. Of course, that did not mean that Booker was going to simply coast through the final portion of the regular season. On March 24th, he dominated the Denver Nuggets in a win while finishing with 49 points and 10 assists. While it was in a loss to the Memphis Grizzlies, Booker went for 41 points as he was entering the playoffs hot.

There is almost no doubt that the finest regular season that Devin Booker has ever had was during the 2021-22 season because that was when he had the number and wins that supported his status as a true elite in the league. Playing only 34 minutes a game, he averaged 26.8 points, 5 rebounds, and 4.8 assists while leading the Phoenix Suns to a league-best record of 64 wins.

Those 64 wins that they had were also the most that the Suns franchise had ever had. Yes, Booker was the franchise player that led the team to its best season ever in terms of wins. And that means a lot because the Suns have had other phenomenal franchise players such as Charles Barkley and Steve Nash who were MVP-caliber.

Speaking of the MVP, Devin Booker finished fourth behind Nikola Jokic, Joel Embiid, and Giannis Antetokounmpo for the award as the league was seeing the return of the dominant big-man position. Nevertheless, he proved himself as one of the best perimeter players in the league because he was given a first team All-NBA slot ahead of the likes of Stephen Curry and Ja Morant.

The fact that the Phoenix Suns were playing the best brand of basketball they have ever played was the reason why they were favorites heading into the playoffs. Of course, they needed to prove themselves capable of going through another tough Western Conference playground before they could claim that they were indeed the best team in the league.

Even though the New Orleans Pelicans were not considered threats in the playoffs after they simply squeaked through the Play-In Tournament, they gave the Suns a lot of trouble in the first round because of the scrappy brand of defense that they played. On top of that, Booker was not available to play in Games 3 and 4 as the Pelicans surprisingly tied the series with two wins apiece heading into Game 5.

Luckily for the Suns, their best player returned in Game 5 to provide more options for Phoenix on offense. While he only scored 13 points in Game 5, his presence was already more than enough to stretch the floor and make the New Orleans defense work harder. As such, the Suns won Game 5 and were within one win away from making it to the second round. After that, the Suns won Game 6 on the strength of the 23 points that Booker contributed. And this win secured a date with the Dallas Mavericks in the second round.

The second-round matchup between the Suns and the Mavs was one of the highlights of the playoffs because it gave rise to a new Western Conference rivalry. Both Devin Booker and Luka Dončić were rising stars in the NBA and were set to be two of the best players the league has to offer for years to come. And that matchup between them was one of the things that fans were eager to see because the two stars were still getting better and better.

In the first two games, the Suns showcased just how hungry they were to return to the Western Conference Finals and even the NBA Finals. Booker had 23 points, 9 rebounds, and 8 assists in a win in Game 1. Then, in Game 2, he led a 20-point win against the Mavs with the 30 points that he contributed. At that time, Dallas had a one-man wrecking crew in Dončić, who the Suns were more than willing to let loose on offense as long as the rest of the Mavs team did not contribute.

However, the Mavericks gave their superstar enough help in Games 3 and 4 to make the series a lot more interesting. Booker had 35 points in Game 4 but the rest of the team did not produce enough to give the team a win. As such, the series went into Game 5 tied 2-2. And the fifth game was when things started to become more interesting in a way that would ultimately be at the expense of the Suns.

In Game 5, Devin Booker and his Phoenix Suns were punishing the Dallas Mavericks on both ends of the floor. It was during a play wherein Booker apparently flopped to get a foul that changed things. As he was lying on the floor for a few more seconds than what was normal, he turned to the camera and said, "The Luka Special." He was referencing how Dončić often got fouls by flopping and overreacting.

Booker finished Game 5 with 28 points and a 30-point win for the Phoenix Suns. His confidence was already through the roof at that point because he and his Suns were only one win away from the Western Conference Finals. But the air apparently changed when Dončić, who was on his way to the locker room, said, "Everybody acting tough when they up." He was obviously referencing the fact that Booker made fun of him with a flop.

While it might be true that the Suns had every opportunity to finish the series after that huge win in Game 5, things did not exactly click for Phoenix in Games 6 and 7. The Dallas Mavericks rallied back from their 3-2 deficit to win Game 6 by 27 points and force Game 7 in Phoenix. Of course, the Suns had homecourt advantage in that series and were supposed to rally together in front of the citizens of the Valley of the Sun. But that was not what happened.

Instead, the Mavericks came out firing on both ends of the floor in Game 7 as Dončić outplayed the entire Suns team in the first half alone. Booker, who had great performances in the playoffs all season long, ended up with a bad night when he shot 3 out of 11 in that poor outing for the Phoenix Suns.

As the dust cleared, the Mavs were headed to the Western Conference Finals with a 33-point win in Game 7. And the Suns were forced to watch the rest of the regular season from their homes after they won 64 games during the regular season and were supposed to be the favorites to make it all the way to the NBA Finals.

Booker and the Suns poked the proverbial bear with their confidence in Game 5 of their series with the Mavs. Dončić and his teammates responded well by delivering two huge blowout wins in Games 6 and 7 to make their opponents eat their words. But while the Suns did not have an entirely successful postseason in 2022 due to the explosive performances from the Mavs, this series against Dallas was the start of a new rivalry between the two teams and their designated franchise players.

In that regard, the NBA was happy enough that a rivalry formed between Booker and Dončić in that 2022 Playoff series. The league tends to feed off rivalries that drive interest in the NBA up. Every decade has its great rivalry, as we saw the likes of Bill Russell vs.

Wilt Chamberlain, Magic Johnson vs. Larry Bird, Michael Jordan vs. The Bad Boys Pistons, and even LeBron James vs. Stephen Curry. As such, this new rivalry between Devin Booker and Luka Dončić might be the rivalry to follow heading into the 2020s. And because they are still relatively young players that are still on the rise, it should be interesting to see how far this rivalry will go.

Despite the fact that the Suns had a disappointing end to that playoff campaign, they were still in a good position to contend in the West because they retained their core group of players. On top of that, Booker was given a four-year, $224 million maximum contract extension that allowed him to bank on the first team All-NBA selection that he earned a season ago.

In that regard, Phoenix started the 2022-23 regular season well enough because the Suns stood at the top of the standings early in the year. Booker, of course, played well for his team as he was consistently putting up 30 or more points. In fact, it was during November that he was able to put up incredible numbers for the Suns, who were looking to contend in the West once more.

On November 18, 2022, Booker finished a narrow loss to the Utah Jazz with 49 points, 8 rebounds, and 10 assists. Then, in a win over the Sacramento Kings on November 28th, he went for 44 points, 8 rebounds, and 6 steals. Booker followed that performance with another scoring outburst in the next game. He went for 51 points in only 31 minutes in a win over the Chicago Bulls as he drained 20 of his 25 shots in that ultra-efficient performance.

Rounding up a fantastic three-game stretch, he finished a loss to the Houston Rockets with 41 points. But his best scoring performance came on December 17th when he had 58 points in a win over the New Orleans Pelicans.

However, Devin Booker went down with a groin injury that kept him out of consecutive games for the Phoenix Suns. While the Suns were able to win games in the past without relying heavily on Booker's ability to score, they slumped hard without him. Phoenix has lost 10 of the 12 games that Booker has thus far missed this season. In that regard, he was clearly the most important player on the roster, as the Suns just cannot seem to put up any points without him on the floor.

It has become clear that the Phoenix Suns of the 2022-23 season are not the same as the team that won 64 games a year ago and went as far as the NBA Finals two seasons ago. Nevertheless, at the time of this writing, they are hopeful that they could right the ship once their best player returns healthy enough to lead them back to a possible playoff appearance.

Of course, the parity between teams during the 2022-23 season is at an all-time high, as teams that were supposed to be contenders have fallen out of the radar, all while some of the younger superstars have started showing why they are the future of the league. And Booker, once he returns, should be able to showcase that he is truly among the players touted as the future of the NBA.

Chapter 5: Personal Life

Devin Booker's parents are Veronica Gutierrez and Melvin Booker. Gutierrez is part Puerto Rican and part Mexican-American. Because of his mother's Puerto Rican roots, Devin can play for Puerto Rico in international tournaments. Meanwhile, Devin's father is of African-American descent and was a decent basketball player himself. Melvin Booker was a standout at Missouri before spending a few seasons as a bench player in the NBA. He later played around the world in various overseas leagues.

Booker has two half-siblings. His older half-brother is Davon Wade, who is about three years older than Devin. The two brothers used to play basketball together when Devin was younger. They would always go to local gyms to play against one another or to challenge neighborhood players.[xxiii] However, when Booker grew up to be bigger and better, Davon could not keep up with his little brother anymore.

Meanwhile, Devin's half-sister, Mya Powell, has Microdeletion Syndrome. He once said that being with his sister helped him become a better man and hopes to one day start a foundation solely for children and young people suffering from the same condition. Since his high school days, Mya has always been his biggest fan and was almost always present at his games.[xxiv]

Whenever Devin is not in the gym or training facility working on his game, he stays at home playing video games. He once said that he and other NBA players would often go online together to play competitively and anonymously because they still love competing in private even when they are outside the basketball court.[xxv]

In July of 2022, Booker was announced as the new cover athlete of the popular NBA 2K video game series. Specifically, he was the featured cover athlete of NBA 2K23, as his cover includes the "Be legendary" quote that Kobe Bryant wrote on his sneakers back in 2016.

Chapter 6: Impact on Basketball

At this point in his career, it is too early to tell what kind of an impact Devin Booker has had on basketball, considering that he is still a 22-year-old player in his fourth season in the NBA. It also does not help that he has been playing for the Phoenix Suns, who have not made any significant noise in the NBA over the past few seasons. Nevertheless, Booker still made something of himself during his first three years in the league and helped propel his team to the postseason and the finals for the first time in many years.

For starters, he has been one of the few shooting guards that play the traditional way. In the NBA today, the role of the shooting guard has drastically decreased. Gone are the days when teams had to rely on the likes of Michael Jordan, Clyde Drexler, Kobe Bryant, Vince Carter, and Allen Iverson for virtually everything they needed to win games. They were scoring, passing, rebounding, and defending.

Now, shooting guards are relegated to roles as catch-and-shoot players that only have to get open by running through screens or by patiently waiting for a pass from their team's penetrators. The first player that fits that mold is Klay Thompson. While he may be an All-Star, he does not rebound or pass as well as shooting guards of the past did. However, he excels in his areas of expertise such as shooting and defending. Bradley Beal is also a player that fits that description very well.

Other than Thompson and Beal, players that do well in that role are guys such as J.J. Redick, Kyle Korver, J.R. Smith, Avery Bradley, and Gary Harris, among others. Only stars such as DeMar DeRozan, Jaylen Brown, Jayson Tatum, and James Harden play like the traditional shooting guards or wings of yesteryear. Even Harden had to switch to point guard to truly make use of his all-around prowess. And that means that the traditional wing guard or small forward has become a rarity in the NBA today.

In a way, Devin Booker has reached the level of all-around excellence that DeRozan, Brown, and Tatum, among others, have reached. Considered a pure shooter coming into the NBA, Booker has risen to become a scorer that can put up points in all three levels of scoring. And after the remarkable finals run season that he had, it can now be argued that he is no longer just a scorer but also a player that can pass, rebound, and defend competitively.

Booker still shoots the ball as well as any other three-point shooter, and he can still score near the basket as well as any designated finisher. But he has added more dimension to that game and is now considered a player that could threaten a team without even scoring. His ability to stretch the floor clearly creates more opportunities for his teammates to get to the basket. That is evidenced by the fact that they struggle to do the same in his absence.

Plus, Booker rebounds well for a shooting guard and makes plays like a true point guard. And even if he is not yet an excellent defender, he has shown significant improvements on that end of the game.

One could say that Devin Booker has now become a good all-around shooting guard but is still far from a finished product. He has mastered the art of being a designated scorer and playmaker and is now one of the true midrange experts of the modern-day NBA. He is similar to the classic wings and shooting guards in the sense that he is capable of playing a good brand of all-around basketball and is capable of putting points up on the board in a hurry.

Other than his profile as a player, Booker has also contributed to basketball one of the highest-scoring performances the NBA has ever seen. In only the 11th time in league history, Booker scored 70 points on his own. Not even Michael Jordan or LeBron James have achieved such a feat. Only Wilt Chamberlain, Kobe Bryant, Elgin Baylor, David Thompson, David Robinson, and Donovan Mitchell have ever scored at least 70 points.

To put it into perspective, six of those performances belong to Wilt Chamberlain. But Wilt was such a dominant player back in the 1960s because the rest of the NBA was not as physically advanced as he was. Eight of those happened in the 1960s and 1970s when the league was not as competitive as it is now. And in the 2000s, only Bryan, Booker, and Mitchell have been able to score at least 70 points in a single game. And it should be noted that all of them did it against more advanced defenses and more physically gifted players in a far more competitive era. That was how amazing Booker's performance truly was.

With that said, Devin Booker is one of the few players to contribute one of the highest-scoring performances in league history. And he did it at such a young age and at a time when he was still developing and improving, whereas all the other players that put up such a performance did it when they were in their primes. Had Booker been a little bit older and more developed on that same night, he might have even gone for 80 or more.

Of course, we also know for a fact that Booker has already done a lot at a comparatively young age. He has yet to enter the prime of his career. Most players tend to enter their prime around the age of 27. Booker has yet to reach that age but he has already become an All-Star multiple times and went to the NBA Finals at the tender age of 24. That means that there are still a lot of things that he can accomplish in the future. And the fact that his game is fundamentally sound means that he can play elite-level basketball for years to come.

Chapter 7: Legacy and Future

Still just entering his prime in the NBA, Devin Booker is now trying to carve his own legacy in the NBA. Sure, he has already become the face of the Suns franchise and is now one of the best scorers the league has to offer. But he has yet to fully stamp his name all over the NBA as a true champion with trophies and individual awards under his belt. Nevertheless, he has already become good enough to carry on the legacies of past players.

As a shooting guard, Booker is well on his way to becoming not only the Phoenix Suns' shooting guard of the future but the NBA's premier shooting guard as well. Ever since the NBA transitioned into a league that relies more on heavy ball movement, outside shooting, and running, the shooting guard has become one of the less-emphasized positions. Most shooting guards today are relegated to the role of a three-and-D player that only takes perimeter shots and defends on the other end.

Because of how the NBA has been evolving and how shooting guards are mostly used for floor spacing and defense, the position has been one of the thinnest concerning star power. Regarded as the best shooting guard in the league, James Harden has been playing mostly as a point guard the last few seasons because of his playmaking prowess. And when it comes to two-way prowess at that position, Klay Thompson was arguably the best. Outside of Harden and

Thompson, there are only a handful of shooting guards that can be called stars in the NBA today.

Despite how the shooting guard position has changed and how teams are not putting the ball in their hands as much as they used to, Devin Booker has risen to become a future star in that role. No other young shooting guard in this league shines brighter than he does, and that is the reason why he might become the best at that position when he finally reaches his peak.

While being the frontrunner of his position among all of the younger players in the league today, Booker also carries the legacy of the great shooting guards that have come before him. He has now earned that mantle, just as Kobe Bryant and Dwyane Wade passed it on to the younger generation of players that owned the wing position. And, as one might already suspect, that mantle once belonged to the legendary Michael Jordan.

With that, Booker is on his way to continuing a legacy of superstardom that started with Jordan's greatness at the shooting guard position. While he does not have the same style of play as His Airness, Booker is the culmination of how the position has evolved to fit the demands and style of today's NBA. He shoots three-pointers at a high level, attacks the basket well for his size and athleticism, and creates his own shots all while making sure he is also rebounding, assisting, and defending. It is a style that is solely almost his own, but it is one that he developed after years of studying and emulating former greats at his position.

Booker also continues the legacy of the select few that have scored 70 or more points in a single game. He joined five others in the elite 70-point club and has scored the most points in a single game in today's generation, just as Kobe Bryant did in his era, and just as David Robinson also did back in the 1990s. It is a legacy that everyone thought would be continued by someone like LeBron James, Kevin Durant, or James Harden. But surprisingly, that mantle was taken up by a young second-year player that had just turned 20 a few months before.

As surprising as that memorable performance was, Booker has a mindset of never putting a limit on his scoring, just as Kobe Bryant always had back in his prime. Because of that, Booker was the first one to score 70 or more points in more than a decade, even though the NBA has superstars that were deemed better scorers and more complete players than he was. He was probably the uncanniest choice to break into the 70-point barrier in this generation, but the crucial fact is that he did it.

But with Devin Booker still improving and developing, he carries an even more important legacy with him—his team's hopes. The Phoenix Suns have been struggling to win a championship ever since the organization's first season in the league. They have also struggled to find players with superstar potential or even capable guys that could help bring the team back to their glory days. But Booker gave them hope because he is one of the true superstars the Suns have had since the days of Nash and Stoudemire.

Though the Suns did not think Booker had a chance of becoming their franchise star when they drafted him, he developed quickly enough to convince the team that he was indeed the face that would take the franchise back to the playoffs. He carries the leadership legacy that once belonged to former Suns greats Steve Nash, Jason Kidd, Kevin Johnson, and Charles Barkley. Along with that, he also carries the hopes of the Phoenix Suns faithful.

All signs point to the possibility that Devin Armani Booker will soon become the leader that will finally take the Phoenix Suns to the promised land. After all, the Suns' front office would not have given him the biggest contract in franchise history had they thought otherwise.

Given his youth and the fact that he is still in the early stages of his career, Booker still has a long way to go before he can truly be called one of the best players in the history of the league. However, he is already one of the best players at his position and has become a true elite in the NBA. In that regard, his innate talent, hardworking mentality, and intelligence have helped and will continue to aid him as he develops into one of the best superstars of today's era. And the scary part is that he has yet to enter his prime.

Devin Booker has just begun to scratch the surface of what may possibly be a deep pool of talent and potential. He is exciting to watch, and a bright ray of hope for the beleaguered Suns. We look forward to great things from this talented young man for years to come.

Final Word/About the Author

I was born and raised in Norwalk, Connecticut. Growing up, I could often be found spending many nights watching basketball, soccer, and football matches with my father in the family living room. I love sports and everything that sports can embody. I believe that sports are one of the most genuine forms of competition, heart, and determination. I write my works to learn more about influential athletes in the hopes that from my writing, you the reader can walk away inspired to put in an equal if not greater amount of hard work and perseverance to pursue your goals. If you enjoyed *Devin Booker: The Inspiring Story of One of Basketball's Rising Shooting Guards,* please leave a review! Also, you can read more of my works on *David Ortiz, Ronald Acuna Jr., Javier Baez, Jose Altuve, Christian Yelich, Max Scherzer, Mookie Betts, Pete Alonso, Clayton Kershaw, Mike Trout, Bryce Harper, Jackie Robinson, Justin Verlander, Derek Jeter, Ichiro Suzuki, Ken Griffey Jr., Babe Ruth, Aaron Judge, Novak Djokovic, Roger Federer, Rafael Nadal, Serena Williams, Baker Mayfield, Josh Allen, Mike Evans, Joe Burrow, Carson Wentz Adam Thielen, Stefon Diggs, Lamar Jackson, Dak Prescott, Patrick Mahomes, Odell Beckham Jr., J.J. Watt, Colin Kaepernick, Aaron Rodgers, Tom Brady, Russell Wilson, Peyton Manning, Drew Brees, Calvin Johnson, Brett Favre, Rob Gronkowski, Andrew Luck, Richard Sherman, Bill Belichick, Candace Parker, Sue Bird, Diana Taurasi, Julius Erving, Oscar Robertson, Ja Morant, Gary Payton, Khris Middleton, Michael Porter Jr., Julius Randle, Jrue Holiday,*

Domantas Sabonis, Mike Conley Jr., Jerry West, Dikembe Mutombo, Fred VanVleet, Jamal Murray, Zion Williamson, Brandon Ingram, Jaylen Brown, Charles Barkley, Trae Young, Andre Drummond, JJ Redick, DeMarcus Cousins, Wilt Chamberlain, Bradley Beal, Rudy Gobert, Aaron Gordon, Kristaps Porzingis, Nikola Vucevic, Andre Iguodala, John Stockton, Jeremy Lin, Chris Paul, Pascal Siakam, Jayson Tatum, Gordon Hayward, Nikola Jokic, Bill Russell, Victor Oladipo, Luka Doncic, Ben Simmons, Shaquille O'Neal, Joel Embiid, Donovan Mitchell, Damian Lillard, Giannis Antetokounmpo, Chris Bosh, Kemba Walker, Isaiah Thomas, DeMar DeRozan, Amar'e Stoudemire, Al Horford, Yao Ming, Marc Gasol, Draymond Green, Kawhi Leonard, Dwyane Wade, Ray Allen, Pau Gasol, Dirk Nowitzki, Jimmy Butler, Paul Pierce, Manu Ginobili, Pete Maravich, Larry Bird, Kyle Lowry, Jason Kidd, David Robinson, LaMarcus Aldridge, Derrick Rose, Paul George, Kevin Garnett, Michael Jordan, LeBron James, Kyrie Irving, Klay Thompson, Stephen Curry, Kevin Durant, Russell Westbrook, Chris Paul, Blake Griffin, Kobe Bryant, Anthony Davis, Joakim Noah, Scottie Pippen, Carmelo Anthony, Kevin Love, Grant Hill, Tracy McGrady, Vince Carter, Patrick Ewing, Karl Malone, Tony Parker, Allen Iverson, Hakeem Olajuwon, Reggie Miller, Michael Carter-Williams, James Harden, John Wall, Tim Duncan, Steve Nash, Gregg Popovich, Pat Riley, John Wooden, Steve Kerr, Brad Stevens, Red Auerbach, Doc Rivers, Erik Spoelstra, Mike D'Antoni and *Phil Jackson* in the Kindle Store. If you love basketball, check out my website at claytongeoffreys.com to join my exclusive list where I let you know about my latest books and give you lots of goodies.

Like what you read? Please leave a review!

I write because I love sharing the stories of influential athletes like Devin Booker with fantastic readers like you. My readers inspire me to write more so please do not hesitate to let me know what you thought by leaving a review! If you love books on life, basketball, or productivity, check out my website at claytongeoffreys.com to join my exclusive list where I let you know about my latest books. Aside from being the first to hear about my latest releases, you can also download a free copy of *33 Life Lessons: Success Principles, Career Advice & Habits of Successful People*. See you there!

Clayton

References

[i] Dauster, Rob. "Devin Booker and his father show the changed landscape of recruiting". *NBC Sports*. 1 August 2013. Web.

[ii] "Mexican roots run deep with the Phoenix Suns". *ESPN*. 11 January 2017. Web.

[iii] "Suns draft pick Devin Booker groomed to play professionally". *Fox Sport*. 26 June 2015. Web.

[iv] Lowe, Zach. "The book on Devin Booker". *ESPN*. 18 March 2015. Web.

[v] Soussi, Omar. "A single decision seven years ago altered career path of Suns' Devin Booker". *Cronkite News*. 7 March 2018. Web.

[vi] Stephenson, Creg. "Moss Point's Devin Booker begins junior season squarely in basketball spotlight". *The Mississippi Press*. 7 November 2012.

[vii] "Booker had a memorable week". *Sun Herald*. 9 December 2012.

[viii] Baumgardner, Nick. "Recruiting: 2014 Michigan target Devin Booker scores 49 points in prep game, Duke now reportedly involved". *MLive*. 24 December 2012. Web.

[ix] Stephenson, Greg. "Moss Point's Devin Booker verbally commits to Kentucky". *The Mississippi Press*. 31 October 2013. Web.

[x] Buhler, John. "John Calipari admits he held Devin Booker back at Kentucky". *Fan Sided*. 13 January 2017. Web.

[xi] *NBADraft.net*. Web.

[xii] *Draft Express*. Web.

[xiii] Strotman, Mark. "Kentucky's Devin Booker could be hidden gem". *NBC Sports*. 8 June 2015. Web.

[xiv] Bickley, Dan. "Suns' Earl Watson plans to win over skeptics". *AZ Central*. 10 May 2016. Web.

[xv] Buha, Jova. "Devin Booker emerges as summer league standout". *ESPN*. 17 July 2016. Web.

[xvi] Coro, Paul. "Suns' Devin Booker to lead summer team, learn from Team USA". *AZ Central*. 8 July 2016. Web.

[xvii] Zirm, Jordan. "Devin Booker's 70-point explosion was inspired by a Kobe Bryant interview". *Stack*. 25 March 2017. Web.

[xviii] Cunningham, Cody. "Devin Booker runs with the summer Suns". *NBA.com*. 5 July 2017. Web.

[xix] King, Dave. "Devin Booker planning to set example for group summer workouts". *SB Nation*. 18 April 2017. Web.

[xx] King, Dave. " The Suns $158 million man getting better this summer — but how much better?". *SB Nation*. 5 August 2015. Web.

[xxi] Cunningham, Cody. "Booker Becomes Fifth Youngest Player to Score

5,000 Career Points". *NBA.com*. 24 January 2019.

xxii Rankin, Duane. "Devin Booker mourning loss of idol, Kobe Bryant". *AZ Central*. 28 January 2020. Web.

xxiii Petersen, Matt. "Booker made family sports his 'own passion'". *NBA.com*. 30 June 2015. Web.

xxiv Gardner, David. " Devin Booker forms unlikely bond with Suns fan". *Sports Illustrated*. 19 May 2016. Web.

xxv Harris, Jarrel. "What's next for the Suns star?". *Sports Illustrated*. 26 April 2017. Web.

Made in the USA
Las Vegas, NV
06 April 2023

70257907R00069